Note to readers
Every effort was made in producing this book to accommodate a
vegetarian diet. Some cheeses are started with animal rennet and
as such are not suitable for vegetarians. For more advice, please
consult individual packages and see page 7.

First published in the United Kingdom in 2019 by
Pavilion
43 Great Ormond Street
London WC1N 3HZ

ISBN 978-1-911641-65-0

A CIP catalogue record for this book is available from the
British Library

10 9 8 7 6 5 4 3 2 1

Reproduction by Mission, Hong Kong
Printed in China

www.pavilionbooks.com

Neither the author nor the publisher can accept responsibility
for any injury or illness that may arise as a result of following the
advice contained in this work. Any application of the information
contained in the book is at the reader's sole discretion.

MOB
VEGGIE

BEN LEBUS

PAVILION

INTRODUCING... 6

INTRODUCING...

What's up Veggie MOB! Welcome to the second MOB Kitchen book, jammed full of the most delicious vegetarian meals you'll ever munch. All for under 20 bucks. All using the freshest ingredients. Same old MOB, veggie-style.

Producing a solely veggie book has been a dream of mine since I started MOB Kitchen. As the MOB has grown, there has been an undeniable enthusiasm surrounding our vegetarian dishes, and it is clear that the people are taking up increasingly meat-free diets. I am a firm believer in vegetarian dishes being as tasty if not tastier than many meat dishes—the thousands of veggie MOB recipe recreations that you send to us really shows this.

MOB Kitchen is committed to being sustainable. The food industry has come under a lot of scrutiny regarding waste and climate change, and we want the *MOB Veggie* cookbook to help promote a change in people's eating habits, whether they are vegetarian or not. At MOB Kitchen, we are determined to do our bit for the environment and with this book, we hope you will be able to as well. With meat-based agriculture accounting for 14.5% of greenhouse gases, it is essential that we cut our meat intake because this is the most significant way in which you can do your bit in preventing climate change. So why not help save our planet while eating delicious food?

While planning and testing the recipes for this book, I realized how easy it is to take up a vegetarian or vegan diet simply by making some clever food swaps. For example, switching your honey for maple syrup or agave. Your butter for veggie margarine. Yogurt for coconut yogurt. Dairy milk for oat milk. And so on. The meat-free products industry is evolving and expanding rapidly, and so making these switches is both easy and affordable.

With the use of battery hen farming still widespread and a continued need to cut down on meat intake, it is time to change the status quo for veggie dishes. People need to be enthusiastic about vegetarian recipes and start to move away from a predominantly meat-based diet. And with that in mind, this book contains both vegetarian and vegan dishes that are as good, if not better, than their meat-based counterparts. We have introduced the wonderful meaty jackfruit that can be bought in a can and makes the Mighty Jackfruit Curry feel so rich you wouldn't even know that it's vegan. Discovering this fruit has opened my eyes to a world of simple, "meaty textured" vegan dishes and there's no looking back! Tofu can be equally as "meaty" and our Black Pepper Tofu is insanely good. There are also our Big Boy Bhaji Burgers, a classic from the MOB—not the predictable bean burger that appears on burger menus as the vegetarian option—this beast goes down an absolute treat.

We've got all of your favorite chapters from the first MOB book, filled with the most delicious veggie and vegan recipes. As with the first book, all we assume you have is salt, pepper, and olive oil. With MOB Classics such as Butternut Squash Pancakes, quick Peri Peri Halloumi Burgers, and Yasai Yaki Udon Noodles, this book has it all. Every single recipe comes with a Spotify code, so that music is at the heart of the experience in each recipe! So start scanning, blast the tunes, and get cooking. As with the first book, every single recipe feeds four people for very little money, busting the myth that delicious veggie dishes come at a higher price.

The book is split into six chapters, starting with Brunch MOB, which brings fresh, unique recipes to the breakfast game. You'll no longer have to pay extra for your veggie fry-up at the fancy café. Second up is Fresh MOB, full of simple salads, soups, and some banging veggie feasts bursting with flavor. Numero three is Speedy MOB. All the recipes take 45 minutes or less, no skill is needed, and they're perfect for lunches or quick suppers. Next we have Fuss-free MOB. At university it was such a pain washing up loads of dishes after a big dinner, so these recipes are mostly one-dish wonders. Easy as 1, 2, 3. The fifth chapter is Flashy MOB. These recipes are a bit more involved; great for a weekend dinner party. So get your MOB over and show them your skills. The final chapter is Fakeout MOB, featuring recipes for fast food, veggie-style, but you can actually do them at home. AND, they are fresher, cheaper, healthier, and much more delicious!

MOB Veggie is the ultimate veggie cookbook, with everything you need to make the perfect vegetarian dishes. Never again will you struggle to cater for your vegan or veggie MOB—this book has it all.

Big love, Ben

All about cheese and condiments

MOB! Watch out for labels on cheese packages to check they are marked as "vegetarian." We use a wide variety of cheeses in the book that are all available as vegetarian-style, so where you see manchego, Parmesan, feta, Gouda, halloumi, mozzarella, goat cheese, pecorino, cream cheese and Cheddar listed, check first that it's veggie! The American Vegetarian Association give many products their seal of approval with the "AVA" label. Make sure you check ingredients like mustards, condiments or curry pastes, too, which sometimes include honey or fish sauce. Keep your eyes peeled for new options. And vegans, there are some fantastic vegan cheeses available to buy that imitate dairy products.

KEY TO SYMBOLS

[★] MOB classic (one of the best-loved recipes from the channel)
[VG] Vegan

When you see one of the following Spotify Codes, you can scan it using the Spotify app to listen to the corresponding playlist/song.

Open 🟢　|　Search 🔍　|　Scan 📷

BRUNCH MOB

INGREDIENTS

6 fresh beets
10 eggs
soy sauce
sesame oil
fresh ginger
fresh cilantro
crushed chilies
2 avocados
1 lime
olive oil
salt and pepper

THE BEST RÖSTIS YOU'LL EVER EAT. KEEP THEM IN THE OVEN UNTIL THEY ARE CRISPY. TRUST US, THEY'LL GET THERE AND IT'S WELL WORTH THE WAIT.

CRISPY ASIAN BEET RÖSTIS [★]

01 Preheat your oven to 400°F.

02 Coarsely grate the fresh beets. Squeeze out the gratings to remove excess moisture. Add to a bowl with 2 eggs and whisk with a fork.

03 Add 2 tablespoons of soy sauce and 1½ teaspoons of sesame oil. Add 2 teaspoons of grated ginger, a handful of chopped cilantro and a teaspoon of crushed chilies. Mix everything together well.

04 Lay some parchment paper on a baking sheet.

05 Divide and shape the rösti mix into eight patties. Lay them on the baking sheet. Bake in the oven for 45 minutes, turning them after 30 minutes.

06 Meanwhile, guac time. Scoop out the avocado flesh and mash in a bowl. Add the juice of a lime and a small handful of chopped cilantro. Add a drizzle of olive oil, and season with salt and pepper. Cover and chill.

07 Egg time. Boil a pan of water. Carefully crack one egg at a time (you'll need eight) into a glass. With a fork or a whisk, create a little whirlpool in the water. Pour the egg into the gently simmering water, not in the center of the whirlpool, but on the edge. The water will fold the white over the yolk and should form a nice little ball. Repeat for the other eggs.

08 Cook each egg for 3 minutes over medium heat. To check if it's done, just gently lift the egg with a spoon. If the white is still a bit wobbly, leave it for 10 more seconds. If it's firm, remove from the pan.

09 Remove the röstis from the oven—they should be nice and crispy at this point.

10 Serve the röstis with a big dollop of guac and a poached egg resting on top of each one. Add a drop or two of sesame oil, sprinkle over some more chopped cilantro and crushed chilies, and then dig in!

CHICKPEA SHAKSHUKA

SERVES 4
45 mins

Nérija
Valleys

INGREDIENTS

2 red bell peppers
2 onions
garlic
fresh cilantro
tomato paste
paprika
ground cumin
hot chili powder
2 x 14-oz. cans of chopped tomatoes
14-oz. can of chickpeas
8 eggs
sourdough bread
1 lemon
vegetable oil
salt and pepper

A ONE-DISH WONDER. ZERO-FUSS. ZERO EFFORT. MAKE SURE YOU FRY THOSE SPICES TO ALLOW THEM TO RELEASE THEIR NATURAL OILS AND REACH THEIR FULL POTENTIAL.

01 Seed and dice your peppers. Dice your onions and 2 garlic cloves. Finely chop some cilantro.

02 Heat a large frying pan or skillet, add a splash of vegetable oil, and throw in your diced veggies. Sauté for 5 minutes, stirring regularly (or until the veggies are softened).

03 Add a tablespoon of tomato paste, some salt and pepper, 1½ teaspoons of paprika, 1½ teaspoons of ground cumin, 1½ teaspoons of chili powder, and a handful of chopped cilantro. Fry for 3 minutes, stirring frequently, allowing the spices to release their flavors.

04 Add the tomatoes to the pan.

05 Drain your chickpeas, rinse them, then add them to the pan. Simmer for 10 minutes on low.

06 Make eight indentations in the chickpea mixture, then add the eggs into the holes and cover with a lid. Wait until the eggs are cooked through.

07 Toast slices of sourdough to serve with it, finish the shakshuka with a squeeze of lemon and some more roughly chopped cilantro. Enjoy.

SPANISH TORTILLA [★]

SERVES 4
45 mins

Reuben James
Shoelace

INGREDIENTS

1 white onion
5 potatoes (ideally with red skins)
10 eggs
4½ oz. pitted green olives
fresh parsley
6-oz. block of manchego
olive oil
salt and pepper

**THE BREAKFAST OF KINGS.
THE MANCHEGO MAKES
THIS. IT'S EXPENSIVE, BUT
WE BUDGETED SO YOU
CAN STILL BUY IT AND
KEEP THE SHOPPING
COST LOW.**

01 Slice the white onion into disks. Halve the disks and then add to a frying pan or skillet with a splash of oil. Fry until soft and slightly browned, and then remove from the pan and set aside.

02 Slice the potatoes into disks. Add them to the pan with another splash of oil, and fry until soft and browned on each side (roughly 5 minutes each side over medium heat). Remove from the heat and set aside.

03 Into a big bowl, crack the eggs. Chop the green olives and add them to the bowl with a handful of chopped parsley (save some for garnish). Whisk this all together and then add your cooked onions and potatoes, and a good sprinkle of salt and pepper. Mix everything together. This is your tortilla mix.

04 Pour some olive oil into a large frying pan or skillet and place over medium–low heat. Pour the tortilla mix into the pan. Crumble three-quarters of the manchego on top. Cook for 15 minutes, occasionally running a spatula around the edge so it doesn't stick.

05 After 15 minutes, remove the pan from the heat, and place a large plate on top of it. In one quick motion, flip the pan over, so the plate is now on the bottom. The tortilla should now be resting on the plate.

06 Place the pan back on the heat. Slide the tortilla off the plate and back into the pan, making sure you push all the bits of potato and onion under the tortilla as you do this.

07 Cook for 5 more minutes on medium–low heat, then remove the pan from the heat. Place the plate back on top, and flip the pan again.

08 Grate over the last of your manchego, and sprinkle over a small handful of chopped parsley. The perfect breakfast.

SERVES 4
1 hr 15 mins

Kansas Smitty's House Band
Beijinhos

INGREDIENTS

1 small butternut squash
self-rising flour
whole milk
2 eggs
Parmesan
fresh rosemary
butter
maple syrup
olive oil
salt and pepper

CHANGING THE BRUNCH GAME FOREVER, THESE PANCAKES ARE THE BUSINESS. THE SWEET AND SAVORY COMBO OF THE CHEESE AND MAPLE SYRUP WORKS A TREAT.

BUTTERNUT SQUASH PANCAKES [★]

01 Preheat your oven to 400°F.

02 Peel, seed, and cut the butternut squash into slices and put on a baking sheet. Drizzle with olive oil and season with salt and pepper. Roast in the oven for 50 minutes.

03 Once the butternut squash is soft, remove it from the oven. Add it to a mixing bowl and mash it up. Sift in scant 2 cups of self-rising flour and mix it all together with a fork. Then add 1½ cups of whole milk, bit by bit. It will be a bit lumpy, but don't worry.

04 Crack in the eggs and add ½ cup grated Parmesan and 1½ teaspoons of chopped rosemary. Season with salt and pepper and mix together. It should be a nice, thick consistency. If needs be, just add a bit more flour.

05 Add some butter to a frying pan, skillet, or pancake pan and allow it to melt and get hot.

06 Add two ladles of your pancake batter to the pan. Cook for 3–4 minutes on each side. Remove the pancakes to a plate and keep warm. Repeat with the remaining mixture.

07 Stack up your pancakes, sprinkle on some more Parmesan, drizzle over some maple syrup, and get stuck in!

INGREDIENTS

2 avocados
1 red onion
fresh cilantro
2 limes
7 oz. radishes
1 red chili
red wine vinegar
14-oz. can of black beans

FETA & BLACK BEAN TACOS WITH HOMEMADE GUAC

01 Scoop the flesh out of the avocados and mash well.

02 Dice the red onion and add half of it to the avocado. Roughly chop some cilantro and add to the mix. Squeeze in the juice of a lime and add salt, pepper, and a splash of olive oil. Mix well, then cover and chill the guac.

03 Thinly slice your whole radishes and your chili (seeded). Add plenty of salt and drizzle with red wine vinegar. Add to the avocado mix but leave a few radishes and chili for garnish.

04 Use a strainer to drain the water from your black beans and rinse them under cold running water. Add to a saucepan along with the other half of your red onion and cook slowly over medium heat with a splash of olive oil for 10 minutes.

garlic
paprika
ground cumin
6 eggs
7-oz. block of feta cheese
8 small tortilla wraps
olive oil
salt and pepper

A GREAT DISH FOR A BIG SHARING BREAKFAST. THIS IS ONE FOR THE HANGOVER.

05 Crush or finely slice 2 garlic cloves and add to the beans along with 1 teaspoon of paprika and 1 teaspoon of ground cumin. Cook for 2–3 minutes. Remove from the heat and cover to keep warm.

06 Crack the eggs into a saucepan and whisk to combine. Add a pinch of salt and pepper and crumble half the feta block into the egg mixture.

07 Scramble your eggs and feta over medium–low heat, stirring and scraping as you go. Be careful not to overcook!

08 Heat your tortillas either in a pan or under the broiler. Just a couple of minutes will do for each one.

09 Assemble your tacos with a spoonful of your spiced black beans, a scoop of your guac, a generous scoop of your feta-scrambled eggs, and the remaining radishes, chili, crumbled feta, and cilantro. Finish with an extra squeeze of lime and a pinch of salt.

VEGGIE NASI GORENG

INGREDIENTS

5 red chilies

garlic

fresh ginger

14 oz. (2¼ cups) basmati rice
(we use Tilda)

4 carrots

2 onions

fresh cilantro

1 white cabbage

soy sauce

sugar

2 limes

4 eggs

vegetable oil

A CLASSIC INDONESIAN FRIED RICE DISH. VEGGIE-FIED. YOU CAN VEGANIZE THIS DISH SIMPLY BY LEAVING OUT THE FRIED EGGS. SOMETHING ABOUT THAT SPICY HIT IN THE MORNING REALLY GETS YOU GOING.

01 Preheat your oven to 475°F.

02 Place four of the red chilies on a lined baking sheet and bake in the oven for 5 minutes.

03 Add 2 unpeeled garlic cloves and a large piece of ginger, then continue to bake for around another 20 minutes, or until the garlic cloves turn sticky, the chilies start to go black, and the ginger is soft. Turn down the heat to 400°F if anything starts to look like it's burning.

04 Meanwhile, put the basmati rice on to cook (according to the package instructions) and prep your veggies. Grate your carrots and a small piece of ginger. Finely slice the onions, 4 garlic cloves, and remaining 1 red chili, and chop up a bunch of the cilantro stalks. Slice up your cabbage into bite-size pieces.

05 Back to the sauce. Cut the roasted chili stalks off, removing the seeds if you want to, and peel the roasted garlic cloves and roasted ginger. Put these, along with 4 tablespoons of soy sauce, 1 teaspoon of sugar, and the juice of a lime into a blender and blend.

06 Pour some vegetable oil into a large frying pan or skillet. Start by frying the onions and garlic on low heat until softened. Then add the cabbage, the grated ginger, and the sliced red chili. Allow to soften and then add the cilantro stalks and the grated carrots.

07 Mix and cook for another 5 minutes, then add your drained rice and the blended sauce.

08 Mix it all together and cook until the sauce is fully mixed in.

09 Meanwhile, fry the eggs in a separate nonstick frying pan.

10 Serve the rice mixture steaming hot, with a squeeze of lime, top each portion with an egg, sprinkle over cilantro leaves, then cut into those runny yolks!

INGREDIENTS

all-purpose flour
chickpea (gram) flour
4 sweet potatoes
1 red onion
garlic
fresh ginger
2 red chilies
fresh cilantro
mustard seeds
fennel seeds
cumin seeds
ground turmeric
1 lime
olive oil
salt and pepper

A DELICIOUS, SPICED ALTERNATIVE TO PANCAKES. YOU WANT TO MASH THE SWEET POTATO A BIT WHEN IT'S IN THE PAN TO MAKE IT NICE AND FLUFFY. IF YOU HAVE TIME, TRY ADDING SOME WILTED GREENS TO YOUR DOSAS FOR AN EXTRA-HEALTHY KICK!

BRUNCH SWEET POTATO DOSAS [VG]

01 Pour ¾ cup of each flour into a large bowl with a generous 1½ cups (13 fl. oz.) of water, and use a whisk to mix the ingredients into a smooth batter. Cover and place in the refrigerator for at least an hour. It will keep for up to 5 days.

02 Preheat your oven to 425°F.

03 Chop your sweet potatoes into cubes, place in a roasting pan, and drizzle with olive oil, then season with salt and pepper. Roast for 30 minutes or until the sweet potato is soft and caramelized.

04 Meanwhile, chop the red onion, 4 garlic cloves, a 1-inch piece of ginger, 1 red chili (seed it first), and some cilantro stalks.

05 Add some olive oil to a frying pan or skillet, then fry 2 teaspoons each of mustard seeds, fennel seeds, and cumin seeds until they are fragrant.

06 Add your chopped onion, garlic, ginger, chili, and cilantro stalks. Fry over low heat until soft. Add a teaspoon of ground turmeric and the roasted sweet potato. Mix everything together well, semi-mashing the sweet potato.

07 Oil a separate frying pan, pour a ladle of batter into the pan and move your ladle in a circular motion to create a thin pancake.

08 Flip and cook so that both sides are golden brown and crispy. Remove the pancakes to a plate. Repeat with the rest of the mixture.

09 Take each dosa, spoon in some sweet potato mixture, and finish with a squeeze of lime juice, more chopped red chili, and some chopped cilantro leaves. Enjoy, MOB!

SERVES 4
50 mins

Tom Misch
Water Baby

INGREDIENTS

1 red onion
garlic
9 oz. cherry tomatoes
3½ oz. pitted olives
capers
dried oregano
2 x 7-oz. blocks of feta cheese
nice ciabatta loaf
fresh parsley
butter
olive oil
salt and pepper

THIS ONE IS PERFECT FOR WHEN YOU HAVE A GROUP OF PEOPLE OVER. LOTS OF TEARING, DIPPING, AND SHARING. THE FETA GOES ALL RICH AND SQUIDGY IN THE OVEN. IT IS SUBLIME.

BAKED FETA, CHERRY TOMATOES & GARLIC CIABATTA

01 Preheat your oven to 350°F.

02 Roughly chop your red onion and a garlic clove.

03 Mix the cherry tomatoes, pitted olives, 4 teaspoons of capers, the chopped onion and garlic, a heaped teaspoon of dried oregano, a drizzle of olive oil, salt and pepper in a bowl.

04 Put the feta blocks on a layer of foil on a baking sheet, folding the edges of the foil up to collect the juices. Pile your tomato mixture on top. Bake in the oven for 30 minutes. When it has baked for 20 minutes, place your ciabatta loaf in the oven to warm up.

05 Meanwhile, chop up 4 garlic cloves and a handful of parsley leaves and add to a bowl. Melt 1¼ sticks butter in a pan and then add to the garlic and parsley. Mix it in.

06 Cut your warm ciabatta in half. Spread your butter all over the two cut sides, and then place back in the oven for 5 minutes.

07 Remove the feta from the oven. Garnish with more chopped parsley. Tear up your garlic ciabatta, spoon out the feta, and tuck in!

4 bagels
salt and pepper
olive oil

**CARAMELIZED ONION &
AVOCADO INGREDIENTS**

butter
4 eggs
9½ oz. Gouda cheese
caramelized onion chutney
2 avocados
arugula

**HALLOUMI & MINT
INGREDIENTS**

8-oz. block of halloumi (or you
can use goat cheese)
fresh mint
plain yogurt
1 lemon
sun-dried tomato paste
arugula

**THE PERFECT SPEEDY
BRUNCH FOR AFTER
A HEAVY NIGHT OUT.
FOLDING THE OMELET
INTO A PACKAGE FOR
THE CARAMELIZED ONION
& AVOCADO BAGEL LETS
THE GOUDA GET NICE
AND GOOEY.**

ULTIMATE BRUNCH BAGELS (2 WAYS)

CARAMELIZED ONION & AVOCADO

01 Heat a teaspoon of butter in a frying pan or skillet until it foams slightly. Crack an egg into a bowl and beat, then season with salt and pepper. Pour the beaten egg into the pan and let cook until you have a thin omelet. Remove to a plate.

02 Slice the Gouda and add a generous amount to the middle of the omelet. Fold the omelet in so that you create a little package. Repeat for the other three eggs.

03 Toast the bagels, then spread with the caramelized onion chutney (as much as you like, to taste).

04 Place an omelet package on top of the chutney, then add some more Gouda, some slices of avocado, and a handful of arugula for good measure. Enjoy!

HALLOUMI & MINT

01 Slice up the block of halloumi and season with a bit of salt and pepper. Pour some olive oil in a pan and fry the halloumi slices until crispy and brown on both sides.

02 Remove some mint leaves from their stalks. Chop up the mint leaves finely and stick them in a bowl. Add 4 tablespoons of plain yogurt and squeeze in the juice of a lemon. Mix.

03 Toast the bagels. Spread some sun-dried tomato paste on the bottom halves, then layer the halloumi, yogurt dressing, and a handful of arugula on top. Replace the toasted top halves. Serve!

VEGAN OVERNIGHT OATS (2 WAYS) [VG]

SERVES 4
4–12 hrs plus prep time

Split Decision Band
Watchin' Out

HEALTHY INGREDIENTS

rolled oats
almond milk
coconut milk
chia seeds
maple syrup
fresh strawberries

BIRCHER INGREDIENTS

jumbo oats
1 red apple
1 green apple
ground cinnamon
almond milk
apple juice (not from concentrate)
almonds (with skins on)
2 bananas
dairy-free coconut yogurt

THESE OATS ARE RIDICULOUSLY EASY TO DO AND A GREAT RECIPE TO HAVE UP YOUR SLEEVE. YOU CAN ADD WHATEVER YOU LIKE—DIFFERENT FRUITS, DIFFERENT NUTS. HAVE FUN AND MAKE IT YOUR OWN.

FOR THE HEALTHY MOB

01 Mix 2 cups of rolled oats, 1 cup of almond milk, 1 cup of coconut milk, 2 tablespoons of chia seeds, and 3–4 tablespoons of maple syrup in a large bowl.

02 Chop 9 oz. of strawberries, then fold them into the mixture, setting some aside in the refrigerator for decorating.

03 Cover, then put in the refrigerator overnight or for at least 4 hours.

04 When ready, divide into four cups and top with the reserved strawberries for texture.

FOR THE BIRCHER-LOVING MOB

01 Pour 3 mugs of oats into a bowl. Grate your apples and add to the oats. Add 2 heaped teaspoons of ground cinnamon, then pour in scant 2½ cups of almond milk and the same of apple juice.

02 Mix everything together, cover in plastic wrap, then put the bowl in the refrigerator overnight.

03 The next morning, chop about ¾ cup of almonds and add them into the bowl with the oat mixture. Mix everything together, then divide it into four bowls. Put a semicircle of banana slices around the edge of each bowl, and spoon on a big dollop of yogurt over the top. Add a pinch of cinnamon, and tuck in!

FRESH MOB

2

SERVES 4
40 mins

Treva Whateva
Singalong

INGREDIENTS

dried green lentils
quinoa
tahini
2 lemons
garlic
red wine vinegar
Dijon mustard
9 oz. cherry tomatoes
1 cucumber
1 Little Gem lettuce
1 avocado
fresh cilantro
fennel seeds
fresh parsley
olive oil
salt and pepper

THIS IS A TEXTURE COMBO MADE IN HEAVEN. CRUNCHY SALAD WITH A RICH, SMOOTH HUMMUS BASE. I GOT INSPIRATION FOR THIS DISH FROM A LUNCH SPOT IN PARIS, AND I'M SO EXCITED FOR YOU ALL TO TRY IT!

QUINOA SALAD WITH GREEN LENTIL HUMMUS BASE [VG]

01   Rinse 1½ cups of green lentils and cook according to the package instructions. Drain and cool.

02   At the same time, 1½ cups of quinoa separately according to the package instructions. Drain, fluff, and set aside to cool.

03   Add your cooked lentils, ⅓ cup of olive oil, ¼ cup of water, ¾ cup of tahini, the juice of a lemon, a peeled garlic clove, and some salt to a food processor and blend until creamy and smooth. Add more olive oil or water to thin out if necessary.

04   Dressing time. Whisk 4 tablespoons of red wine vinegar, 2 tablespoons of Dijon mustard, a pinch of salt, and a good grinding of pepper. Slowly add ⅓ cup of olive oil to the mixture while whisking. Then add the juice of a lemon.

05   Halve the cherry tomatoes, and chop up the cucumber, lettuce, and scooped avocado flesh. Finely chop the cilantro.

06   Mix together the salad veggies and quinoa, and pour over a cup of the dressing. Store the leftover dressing in the refrigerator for up to 2 days. Sprinkle with fennel seeds and some parsley. Toss together.

07   Create a green lentil hummus base on a serving plate, then add the salad on top. Enjoy!

INGREDIENTS

fresh ginger
red miso paste
7 oz. purple sprouting broccoli
dried vermicelli noodles
beansprouts
3 limes
soy sauce
fresh cilantro
1 cucumber
1 red chili
salted peanuts
olive oil

THE ROASTED MISO BROCCOLI. THE SALTY PEANUTS. THE ZINGY DRESSING. ALL COMING TOGETHER TO FORM ONE OF THE MOST SPECTACULAR MOUTHFULS YOU'RE EVER LIKELY TO TASTE.

VIETNAMESE VERMICELLI BOWL [VG]

01 Preheat your oven to 400°F.

02 Finely chop a 1-inch piece of ginger. Mix 1½ tablespoons of miso paste with some olive oil in a bowl. If necessary, add up to 3 tablespoons of water to loosen the mixture.

03 Wash your broccoli and place in a roasting pan, then baste with the miso mixture. Let it roast in the oven for 30 minutes.

04 Meanwhile, cook 14 oz. of vermicelli according to the package instructions. Drain and rinse with cold water until the noodles are cold.

05 Wash your beansprouts and lightly pan-fry with a splash of olive oil until slightly wilted. Set to the side to cool.

06 Dressing time. Take 3 limes and use a teaspoon to get all the juice out. Add 2 teaspoons of soy sauce. Chop up a handful of cilantro and mix in.

07 Chop your cucumber into circles and then cut the circles into halves.

08 Seed your red chili and finely chop it. Chop up another handful of cilantro.

09 Assemble your bowls with vermicelli, broccoli, and beansprouts, then pour a generous amount of dressing on top of each portion, top with the cucumber, chili, cilantro, and crushed salted peanuts. Tuck in!

SERVES 4
30 mins

Oby Onyioha
Enjoy Your Life

INGREDIENTS

8 oz. broccolini
14 oz. (2¼ cups) long-grain
brown rice
tahini
sesame oil
1 lemon
1 mango
pickled ginger
salted peanuts
mixed sesame seeds

WE SPENT A LONG
TIME DEVELOPING A
COMPLETELY VEGAN
POKE BOWL, AND
HERE IT IS. A BITE OF
THE TAHINI-DRESSED
GRIDDLED BROCCOLINI
IS LIKE DYING AND GOING
TO HEAVEN. SHOUT OUT
TO ISLAND POKE FOR
THE INSPIRATION.

POKE BOWL WITH GRIDDLED TAHINI BROCCOLINI [★] [VG]

01 Chop the broccolini into bite-size pieces. Add to a pan of boiling water and boil for 4 minutes. Drain.

02 Put the brown rice on to cook (following the package instructions).

03 Meanwhile, heat a griddle (ridged stovetop) pan. Add the broccolini to the pan. Cook until charred. Remove and set aside.

04 Dressing time. Add 3 tablespoons of tahini, a teaspoon of sesame oil, and the juice of a lemon into a bowl. Add water and mix until you have a creamy consistency.

05 Add the broccolini to the dressing and toss it around.

06 Once the rice is ready, drain, and then add 2 teaspoons of sesame oil to it. Toss it in.

07 Peel, pit, and cut the mango into chunks.

08 Serving time. Fill the bottom of four bowls with rice. Add equal portions of broccolini and mango chunks to each bowl. Finish with a handful of pickled ginger in each bowl.

09 Crush up some salted peanuts and scatter them on top, along with some sesame seeds. Dig your fork in and enjoy!

SERVES 4

1 hr

The Gene Dudley Group

Inspector Norse

INGREDIENTS

2 bell peppers (1 red, 1 yellow)
pine nuts
fresh basil
1 lemon
garlic
Parmesan
3 zucchinis
8 oz. halloumi (use goat cheese
if you can't find halloumi)
all-purpose flour
2 eggs
dried breadcrumbs
9 oz. cherry tomatoes
arugula
olive oil
vegetable oil
salt and pepper

HALLOUMI CROÛTONS. THE GREATEST INVENTION SINCE SLICED BREAD. CRUNCHY OUTSIDE, WITH THAT BEAUTIFUL SOFT HALLOUMI BITE ON THE INSIDE. LEAVE THE HALLOUMI TO COOK UNTIL THE BREADCRUMBS ARE A DEEP BROWN.

HALLOUMI CROÛTON SUPER SALAD [★]

01   Preheat your oven to 400°F.

02   Seed and cut your bell peppers into chunks. Add to a roasting pan with salt, pepper, and a drizzle of olive oil. Roast in the oven for 40 minutes or until charred and soft.

03   Meanwhile, pesto time. First toast scant ½ cup of pine nuts in a dry frying pan or skillet. Into a blender add scant ¼ cup of the toasted pine nuts, a handful of basil leaves, the juice of a lemon, 1 peeled garlic clove, and scant ½ cup of grated Parmesan. Add 5 tablespoons of olive oil and blend until smooth.

04   Zucchini time. Cut your zucchinis into thin strips. Drizzle with olive oil, salt, and pepper. Add to a hot griddle (ridged stovetop) pan and cook for 5–6 minutes on each side.

05   Halloumi croûton time. Cut your halloumi into small cubes. Get three bowls out. Add flour to one, 2 eggs to another (whisk them up), and breadcrumbs to the third. Dip your halloumi in the flour, then the eggs, then the breadcrumbs.

06   Put a pan on the heat. Fill it up to ¾ inch depth with vegetable oil. Heat the oil until hot, and then add the croûtons to the pan. Cook for 3–4 minutes until golden brown.

07   Remove the croûtons from the heat and drain them on some paper towels.

08   Halve your cherry tomatoes.

09   Add all of your ingredients, along with a bag of arugula and the leftover pine nuts, to a large salad bowl. Pour over your pesto dressing, toss it all together, and serve it up.

ROMESCO PAPPARDELLE WITH KALAMATA OLIVES

INGREDIENTS

4 red bell peppers
garlic
1 lemon
slivered almonds
sherry vinegar
tomato paste
1 lb. 2 oz. dried pappardelle
Kalamata olives
fresh basil
olive oil
salt and pepper

01 Preheat your oven to 350°F.

02 Add the red peppers and 3 garlic cloves (skin on) to a roasting pan with a lemon cut in half. Roast in the oven for 45 minutes.

03 Once the peppers are soft, remove the stalk and add them to a blender. Squeeze in the roasted garlic pulp and roast lemon juice. Add 2 tablespoons of slivered almonds, 2 tablespoons of sherry vinegar, a tablespoon of tomato paste, salt, pepper, and 3 tablespoons of olive oil. Whiz until smooth.

04 Put the pasta on to cook (following the package instructions).

05 Once the pasta is al dente, drain (save some of the pasta water). Add back to the pan with your Romesco sauce, a large handful of chopped Kalamata olives, and a handful of torn basil. Toss to mix. Serve the pasta into bowls, garnish with some more basil, and enjoy!

ROMESCO SAUCE—A NUT-BASED CATALAN RECIPE. ITS SAVORY, RICH FLAVOR WORKS PERFECTLY WITH PASTA AND SOME SALTY KALAMATA OLIVES. A GREAT SIMPLE PASTA DISH TO ADD TO YOUR REPERTOIRE.

BABA GANOUSH PITAS

SERVES 4
1 hr 10 mins

Junodream
Fire Doors

INGREDIENTS

3 eggplants
garlic
3 beets
1 carrot
fresh mint
fresh cilantro
8 oz. halloumi (or you can use goat cheese if you can't find halloumi)
tahini
2 lemons
8 pitas
salt and pepper

01 Preheat your oven to 400°F.

02 Add the whole eggplants to a roasting pan. Add 2 garlic cloves to the pan (in their skins).

03 Roast in the oven for an hour, making sure the eggplants are cooked all the way through.

04 While the eggplants are cooking, grate your beet and carrot. Chop up a handful each of mint and cilantro and mix into the grated veggies.

05 Slice your halloumi and pan-fry it in a hot, dry pan, letting the slices get crisp and brown all over.

06 Remove the eggplants from the oven. Slice them open and scoop out the soft flesh. Squeeze out the roasted garlic pulp from their skins. Put the eggplant flesh and garlic into a food processor with 2 tablespoons of tahini, the juice of a lemon, and salt and pepper. Process until smooth.

07 Toast your pitas. Spread a dollop of baba ganoush on the inside of each pita, stuff it with halloumi slices and grated veggies, and squeeze some lemon juice to top it off. Tuck in!

BABA GANOUSH—PROBABLY ONE OF THE BEST THINGS IN THE WORLD. SOFT, GARLICKY, SMOKY EGGPLANT. IT GOES WITH JUST ABOUT ANYTHING. WE HAVE DECIDED TO STUFF IT INSIDE A PITA WITH A CRUNCHY SALAD FOR THE ULTIMATE SANDWICH.

INGREDIENTS

7 oz. dried soba noodles
9 oz. portobello mushrooms
soy sauce
2 carrots
½ red cabbage
1 red bell pepper
1 lime
sriracha sauce
sesame oil
½ oz. nori seaweed
fresh cilantro
olive oil

THIS IS DEFINITELY ONE FOR THE HEALTHY MOB—SOBA NOODLES ARE SAINTLY. MAKE SURE YOU LEAVE THE MUSHROOMS COOKING UNTIL THEY ARE DARK AND GNARLY—THEY BRING THE DEPTH OF FLAVOR HERE.

SOBA NOODLE SALAD WITH CHARRED PORTOBELLO MUSHROOMS [VG]

01 Cook the soba noodles according to the package instructions. Drain and rinse with cold water (to stop them overcooking).

02 Finely slice the portobello mushrooms and add to a frying pan or skillet with a splash of olive oil. Add a tablespoon of soy sauce, and cook the mushrooms until they begin to char. Remove from the heat.

03 Grate the carrots and shred the red cabbage, and seed and finely slice the red pepper. Mix with the noodles.

04 Sauce time. Whisk together 2 tablespoons of soy sauce, the juice of a lime and a tablespoon of sriracha. Add 3 tablespoons of sesame oil while whisking.

05 Combine the dressing and the noodles, top with the mushrooms, and sprinkle over the nori seaweed (broken into little pieces) and a handful of chopped cilantro. Serve up.

INGREDIENTS

12 new potatoes (big ones)
2 red bell peppers
1 red onion
2 lemons
2 corn on the cob
garlic
dried oregano
red wine vinegar
2 hot red chilies
14-oz. can of black beans
7-oz. block of feta cheese
½ cucumber
fresh cilantro
olive oil
salt and pepper

IF YOU THOUGHT YOU COULDN'T EAT GOOD PERI PERI OUTSIDE OF PORTUGAL, YOU'RE VERY, VERY WRONG. WE HAVE PERFECTED OUR RECIPE, WHICH WORKS PERFECTLY ON TOP OF THESE CRISPY HASSELBACK POTATOES.

HASSELBACK POTATOES WITH PERI PERI DRESSING & FETA

01 Preheat your oven to 400°F.

02 Prep the potatoes. Carefully make small vertical slits, 1/16 inch apart, three-quarters of the way down each potato, all the way along.

03 Add the potatoes to a roasting pan. Drizzle with olive oil and season well with salt and pepper. Roast in the oven for 50 minutes or until golden and crispy.

04 Peri peri time. In another roasting pan, add the seeded, roughly sliced red peppers, the sliced red onion, and 1 lemon (halved, cut-side down). Drizzle with olive oil and put the pan into the oven for 45 minutes.

05 Meanwhile, add your corn to another roasting pan, drizzle with olive oil, season with salt and pepper, and roast in the oven for 30 minutes, turning every 10 minutes.

06 Once the potatoes are nice and crispy, remove them from the oven and set aside.

07 Peri-peri sauce time. Add your roasted peppers, onion, and pulp from the lemon to a blender. Add 2 grated garlic cloves, 2 teaspoons of dried oregano, 1½ tablespoons of red wine vinegar, the chilies, salt, pepper, and a drizzle of olive oil. Add the zest and juice of a fresh lemon. Whiz together to make your smooth sauce.

08 Remove the corn from the oven. Slice the corn kernels from the cobs and drain and rinse the black beans. Chop up the cucumber and mix with the beans and the corn kernels, a handful of chopped coriander, the juice of half a lemon, a little olive oil, salt, and pepper.

09 Load the potatoes with the sauce and add the crumbled feta. Scatter chopped cilantro on top and serve up with the corn salad on the side.

SIMPLE CHIMICHURRI, ROASTED PEPPER & NEW POTATO SALAD

SERVES 4
55 mins

Odyssey
Hang Together

INGREDIENTS

4 mixed bell peppers
(not green)
1 lb. 7 oz. new potatoes
fresh cilantro
fresh parsley
red wine vinegar
1 red chili
3 shallots
dried oregano
garlic
manchego
olive oil
salt and pepper

THIS DISH IS MORE OF AN ASSEMBLY THAN A RECIPE—ALL THE ELEMENTS JUST WORK SO WELL TOGETHER. THE SALTY MANCHEGO SHAVINGS ON THE TOP MAKE ALL THE DIFFERENCE.

01 Preheat your oven to 350°F.

02 Seed and quarter the bell peppers and add to a roasting pan. Season with salt and pepper and drizzle with olive oil. Put the pan in the oven for 45 minutes.

03 Bring a pan of water to a boil. Add a large pinch of salt and then add your potatoes. Cook until soft.

04 Meanwhile, chimichurri time. Add a large handful of chopped cilantro and chopped parsley to a bowl. Add 4 tablespoons of red wine vinegar, 1 seeded and finely chopped red chili, 7 tablespoons of olive oil, the chopped shallots, a heaped teaspoon of the oregano, and salt and pepper. Add a grated garlic clove and mix everything together. It should be the consistency of pesto, so add more herbs if needed. Set aside.

05 Once cooked, drain, and then add salt, pepper, and olive oil to the potatoes.

06 Serving time. Into each bowl add some roasted peppers, some potatoes, and then cover with a few large dollops of chimichurri. Shave manchego over the top and tuck in!

INGREDIENTS

4 red or yellow bell peppers
ciabatta
dried chili flakes
garlic
4 beef tomatoes
2 mozzarella balls
balsamic vinegar
fresh basil
olive oil
salt and pepper

A NAUGHTY, NAUGHTY LITTLE SALAD. IDEAL FOR THE LONG SUMMER EVENINGS. THE GARLIC CROÛTONS ARE GREAT AND CAN BE USED TO ELEVATE ALL OF YOUR SALADS.

TOMATO & ROASTED PEPPER SUMMER SALAD

01 Preheat your oven to 400°F.

02 Seed and slice your red or yellow peppers into thin strips and season with salt and pepper.

03 Place on a baking sheet lined with parchment paper, drizzle with olive oil, and roast in the oven for 15–20 minutes.

04 Cut a small loaf of ciabatta into small chunks. Add to another baking sheet. Drizzle with olive oil. Add 2 teaspoons of chili flakes and 2 crushed garlic cloves and mix around. Roast for 30 minutes until a deep golden brown.

05 Slice the tomatoes and tear the mozzarella into big chunks.

06 Combine in a large bowl and add a large splash of olive oil, some salt and pepper, and a smaller splash of balsamic vinegar. Mix well.

07 Add the roasted peppers to the tomato and mozzarella mixture. Mix well.

08 Serve your fresh salad in bowls and sprinkle your crunchy croûtons on top. Garnish with fresh basil leaves and a pinch of salt.

3

SPEEDY MOB

VEGGIE SATAY NOODLES

SERVES 4
20 mins

Metronomy
The Look

INGREDIENTS

3 bell peppers
2 carrots
sesame oil
14 oz. dried egg noodles
6 scallions
1 lime
peanut butter
14-oz. can of coconut milk
soy sauce
fresh cilantro
peanuts
vegetable oil
salt

**DONE IN ABOUT
20 MINUTES, SO A
PERFECT MIDWEEK
SUPPER. MAKE SURE
YOU SCRUNCH YOUR
SCALLIONS TO GET THEM
PICKLING—THIS SPEEDY
LIMEY PICKLE BRINGS
THE FRESH KICK
THAT IS NEEDED.**

01 Seed your peppers and chop them into matchsticks. Do the same for the carrots. Add both to a wok with a splash of vegetable oil. Cook on high so they start charring. Once the vegetables are charred but still firm, remove them from the heat. Add them to a bowl and add 1½ teaspoons of sesame oil. Toss to mix.

02 Put the egg noodles on to cook in a separate pan and cook according to the package instructions.

03 Finely chop your scallions and add them to a bowl. Squeeze over the juice of a lime and add a big pinch of salt. Scrunch everything together—this will pickle the scallions and take away the strong flavor.

04 Back to the wok. First, wipe out the excess oil. Then add a tablespoon of peanut butter, the coconut milk, and 4 tablespoons of soy sauce. Mix everything together and bubble over high heat until you have a nice, thick sauce.

05 Drain the noodles and pour them into the wok. Add the sesame vegetables and stir everything together.

06 Tip in your scallions, add a teaspoon more of sesame oil and mix everything together. Scatter in some chopped cilantro and peanuts, and serve up!

PERI PERI HALLOUMI BURGERS [★]

SERVES 4
45 mins

Donnell Pitman
Love Explosion

INGREDIENTS

3 mixed bell peppers
(not green)
1 red onion
½ lemon
smoked paprika
dried oregano
red wine vinegar
red chili

01 Preheat your oven to 400°F.

02 Seed the peppers and cut them and your red onion into chunks. Put them on a baking sheet. Place the lemon half, face down, onto the sheet. Roast in the oven for 45 minutes.

03 Once the peppers are beginning to char, remove the sheet. Add one-third of the pepper and onion mixture (reserve the rest) and the pulp of the roast lemon to a blender, with a teaspoon each of smoked paprika and dried oregano. Add 1 tablespoon of red wine vinegar, a seeded red chili, and a peeled garlic clove. Season with salt and pepper and add a tablespoon of olive oil. Whiz until smooth.

04 Slice your halloumi, then get it on a hot griddle (ridged stovetop) pan. Cook for 3–4 minutes on each side.

05 Split and toast your burger buns.

garlic
1 lb. halloumi (or you can
use goat cheese if you can't
find halloumi)
4 burger buns
mayonnaise
bag of salad greens
olive oil
salt and pepper

06 Mix your blended peri peri sauce with 5 tablespoons of mayonnaise.

07 Assembly time. Take each bun. Add a layer of peri peri mayo, some of the roasted peppers, then some halloumi, followed by some salad greens, more mayo, then top it with the bun lid. Tuck in and enjoy!

THE FRESHEST VEGGIE BURGER ABOUT. THE PERI-PERI MAYO IS EVERYTHING—LATHER IT ON GENEROUSLY!

YASAI YAKI UDON NOODLES [★] [VG]

SERVES 4
20 mins

Rex Orange County
Loving Is Easy

INGREDIENTS

5½ oz. portobello mushrooms
4½ oz. fresh shiitake
mushrooms
1 onion
1 carrot
white cabbage
5 scallions
sesame oil
14 oz. wok-ready udon noodles
soy sauce
mirin
vegetable oil
pepper

01 Slice up the portobello and shiitake mushrooms. Finely chop the onion. Cut the carrot into matchsticks. Shred ⅓ of a white cabbage. Finely slice 3 of the scallions.

02 Into a pan add 2 tablespoons of sesame oil and 2 tablespoons of vegetable oil.

03 Add your carrot, cabbage, and onion. Allow them to soften for 2–3 minutes, and then throw in your portobello mushrooms.

04 Cook for another minute, then add your shiitake mushrooms. Mix everything in, and cook for another 2 minutes.

05 At this point, add your 3 sliced scallions. Cook for another 2 minutes and then add the udon noodles. Season with pepper and then add 4 tablespoons of soy sauce and 2 tablespoons of mirin.

06 Mix everything together, cook for another minute, then you're all set. Remove from the heat, and serve while hot. Garnish with a the remaining 2 sliced scallions and enjoy!

A RESTAURANT CLASSIC THAT IS SO SIMPLE TO DO AT HOME YOURSELVES. MIRIN IS KEY IN THIS DISH—YOU MAY HAVE TO GO TO A BIGGER OR SPECIALIST STORE TO FIND IT, BUT IT IS ESSENTIAL AND WORTH THE EFFORT. IT IS JAPANESE RICE WINE, AND BRINGS THE EDGE.

SERVES 4

20 mins

Hailu Mergia
Tizita

INGREDIENTS

1 lb. 2 oz. gnocchi
9 oz. chestnut mushrooms
butter
garlic
fresh rosemary
fresh thyme
1 lemon
crème fraîche or sour cream
7 oz. goat cheese
salt and pepper

GOAT CHEESE IS THE ULTIMATE CHEESY TOPPING HERE. FOR EXTRA FLAVOR, FINISH IT UNDER THE BROILER UNTIL NICE AND GOLDEN.

CREAMY MUSHROOM GNOCCHI WITH GOAT CHEESE

01 Put a large pan of water on to boil, add a generous amount of salt and cook the gnocchi according to the package instructions.

02 Thinly slice the chestnut mushrooms.

03 Melt a tablespoon of butter in a large frying pan or skillet over medium heat.

04 Add the sliced mushrooms and cook until soft (3–5 minutes). At this point, add a crushed clove of garlic and a small handful of rosemary and thyme leaves, and the zest of half a lemon. Cook for another minute.

05 Add a tablespoon of crème fraîche or sour cream. Stir it through the mushrooms.

06 Squeeze in 10 drops of freshly squeezed lemon juice.

07 When your gnocchi's cooked, drain and add to your sauce. Toss to mix.

08 Dollop the goat cheese over the top. Season well with pepper and serve warm. If making in advance, you could transfer the whole lot to a baking dish and warm up under a low broiler before serving.

SERVES 4
45 mins

Tom Grennan
Praying

INGREDIENTS

1 onion
garlic
fresh ginger
tomato paste
ground cumin
paprika
dried chili flakes
generous 2 cups split red
lentils
14-oz. can of coconut milk
fresh spinach
14 oz. (2¼ cups) basmati rice
olive oil

SPICY COCONUT LENTIL DAL [VG]

01   Chop up your onion, 3 garlic cloves, and a thumb-size piece of ginger.

02   Pan-fry the onion, garlic, and ginger in a little oil. When soft, add a good tablespoon of tomato paste, 1 teaspoon of ground cumin, 1 teaspoon of paprika, and 1 teaspoon of chili flakes. Fry for a couple of minutes to release their aromas.

03   Add the lentils and coconut milk, and bring to a boil, then reduce the heat and simmer for 30 minutes, adding water when necessary and stirring frequently.

04   Stir in some spinach right at the end.

05   Meanwhile, put the basmati rice on and cook according to the package instructions. Drain.

06   Serve the dal over the rice with extra chili.

THIS IS THE ULTIMATE WINTER WARMER. I HAVE ALWAYS BEEN A BIT SKEPTICAL ABOUT LENTILS, BUT THEY ARE THE ABSOLUTE HERO IN THIS DISH. SO RICH. SO WARMING. GIVE IT A GO...

15-MINUTE LAKSA [VG]

SERVES 4
15 mins

Rahaan
Make Me Hot

INGREDIENTS

ground coriander
paprika
ground cumin
4 red chilies
1 onion
2 lemongrass stalks
fresh ginger
garlic

01 Make the paste first—add 1 teaspoon each of ground coriander, paprika, and ground cumin to a pan and heat until fragrant (1 minute or so). Add to a food processor with the red chilies (seeded), the roughly chopped onion, the lemongrass stalks (white part only), a small grated piece of ginger, 2 peeled garlic cloves, and a splash of vegetable oil. Whiz to combine.

02 Add the paste to a saucepan and fry for a few minutes.

03 Meanwhile, finely slice the carrots and slice the zucchinis.

04 Add your vegetables and coconut milk to the pan and bring to a boil, then add 5½ oz. rice stick noodles. Cook until the noodles are soft.

05 Turn off the heat, add some sliced sugar snap peas, a handful of chopped cilantro, and squeeze the lime over the top.

06 Serve up and enjoy!

2 carrots
2 zucchinis
2 x 14-oz. cans of coconut milk
dried rice stick noodles
sugar snap peas
fresh cilantro
1 lime
vegetable oil

MAKING YOUR OWN LAKSA PASTE IS THE
EASIEST THING TO DO AND PACKS SO MUCH
MORE FLAVOR THAN THE STORE-BOUGHT STUFF.
DONE IN MINUTES—GIVE IT A SPIN AND
IMPRESS YOUR MOB.

INGREDIENTS

1 onion
2 carrots
2 eggplants
2 zucchinis
garlic
2 x 14-oz. cans of chopped
tomatoes
French lentils
dried oregano
dried thyme
ground coriander
fresh basil
olive oil
salt and pepper

**SO GOOD IT'S ALMOST AS
IF I HAD A RAT IN MY HAT
WHEN I WAS MAKING IT...**

QUICK LENTIL RATATOUILLE [VG]

01 Finely dice the onion and carrots, add to a pan with a splash of olive oil, and cook until the onions are soft and translucent. Then add the eggplants and the zucchinis, both cut into rough cubes, and cook down until the eggplants and zucchinis start to char.

02 Finely chop 3 garlic cloves, add to the pan, and stir well. Once soft, add your cans of tomatoes. Cook for 8 minutes over medium heat.

03 Add scant 2 cups of rinsed French lentils, generous 2 cups of water, 1 teaspoon of dried oregano, ½ teaspoon of dried thyme, 1 teaspoon of ground coriander, and salt and pepper. Simmer over low heat for 20 minutes, stirring frequently to make sure the lentils are not sticking. Add a little water if and when necessary.

04 Once you have a delicious, thick ratatouille, add a handful of fresh basil leaves. Serve in bowls with salt and pepper sprinkled on top.

PUMPKIN PASTA [VG]

SERVES 4
45 mins

The Kinks
Victoria

INGREDIENTS

1 pumpkin
1 sweet potato
garlic
2 red onions
1 lb. 2 oz. dried spaghetti
3 leeks
olive oil
salt and pepper

PUMPKIN AND LEEKS—A MATCH MADE IN HEAVEN. THE TRICK WITH LEEKS IS TO COOK THEM ON LOW–MEDIUM HEAT SO THEY GET REALLY NICE AND SILKY WITHOUT CATCHING ON THE PAN.

01   Preheat your oven to 425°F.

02   Cut your pumpkin up, seed it, and put it in a roasting pan with some olive oil, salt, and pepper.

03   Wash and cut the sweet potato, 2 garlic cloves, and the onions, then place in a separate roasting pan with olive oil, salt, and pepper.

04   Roast both pans for around 30 minutes, making sure to take out the garlic as soon as it looks caramelized because it tends to burn.

05   Meanwhile, cook the pasta according to the package instructions.

06   Wash and slice the leeks, then pan-fry with a splash of olive oil and a generous amount of salt.

07   Back to the roasted vegetables. Place all of them into a blender and blend until smooth. Combine the drained pasta and blended sauce in a pan, making sure the sauce covers all the pasta. Serve with a drizzle of olive oil and a spoonful of leeks on top. Season with pepper and serve!

30-MINUTE PEANUT RED THAI CURRY BOWLS [VG]

SERVES 4
30 mins

The Avener
Fade Out Lines
(The Avener Rework)

INGREDIENTS

5 shallots
3 red chilies
paprika
fresh ginger
fresh cilantro
2 limes
garlic
lemongrass paste
14 oz. (2¼ cups) basmati rice
(we use Tilda)
2 red bell peppers
1 large carrot
14-oz. can of coconut milk
peanut butter
olive oil

01 First, make your curry sauce. Into a blender add the shallots, chilies (seeded), 3 teaspoons of paprika, a chopped 2-inch piece of ginger, a handful of fresh cilantro including stalks, the juice of a lime (use a teaspoon to get all the juice out), 2 garlic cloves, and 3 heaped teaspoons of lemongrass paste. Whiz until smooth.

02 Put the basmati rice on to cook (following the package instructions).

03 Seed and chop up your bell peppers. Chop up the carrot.

04 In a pan, add a splash of olive oil and throw in your chopped carrot and chopped red peppers.

05 When mostly cooked through, add your prepared curry sauce. Mix thoroughly.

06 Add your coconut milk and allow it to simmer so that the sauce thickens.

07 When your sauce is thick enough, add 2 generous teaspoons of peanut butter and fold it in.

08 Serve on a bed of drained rice and top with extra fresh cilantro and a squeeze of lime.

DITCH ALL THOSE STORE-BOUGHT SAUCES FOREVER—THIS IS THE WAY FORWARD. IF POSSIBLE, USE PEANUT BUTTER MADE FROM PEANUTS ONLY—THE BEST STUFF REALLY TAKES THIS DISH TO THE NEXT LEVEL. MOST PEANUT BUTTER IS VEGAN BUT WATCH OUT FOR ONES THAT USE HONEY.

RAINBOW DRAGON NOODLES

SERVES 4
25 mins

MR Given Raw
Boogie Magic

INGREDIENTS

4 zucchinis
2 carrots
1 red cabbage
2 red bell peppers
sriracha sauce
soy sauce
sugar
4 eggs
unsalted cashews
fresh cilantro
vegetable oil
salt

A HEALTHY NOODLE OPTION—PACKED FULL OF VEGGIES. A GREAT LIGHT DINNER. ADD SOME COOKED DRIED NOODLES IF YOU WANT TO BULK IT OUT!

01 Spiralize the zucchinis and carrots. Finely slice the red cabbage and seed and finely slice the red peppers.

02 Sauce time. In a bowl, mix together 5 teaspoons of sriracha, 4 tablespoons of soy sauce, and a teaspoon of sugar. Set to the side.

03 Add all the vegetables to a frying pan or skillet with a good splash of vegetable oil. Fry for 1 minute, and then add the beaten eggs to the pan.

04 Let cook until the egg starts to form around the veggie noodles and then mix well. Add the sauce! Mix in.

05 In a separate frying pan or skillet, toast some unsalted cashews with some salt.

06 Serve the rainbow noodles with the toasted cashews and some chopped cilantro.

FUSS-FREE MOB

4

SERVES 4
15 mins

Will Sessions
Come on Home

INGREDIENTS

1 cucumber
1 red bell pepper
1 green bell pepper
garlic
3 scallions
1 stale bread roll
14 plum tomatoes
sherry vinegar
olive oil
salt and pepper
ice

DITCH THE CARTON STUFF. THIS EASY RECIPE IS THE BUSINESS—AND SO, SO REFRESHING. GET SOME NICE, RIPE TOMATOES.

HOMEMADE GAZPACHO [★] [VG]

01 Prep time. Peel, seed, and slice the cucumber. Seed the red and green peppers, and chop into chunks. Chop 1½ garlic cloves into thin slices. Slice up the scallions. Tear up the stale bread roll.

02 Throw all these ingredients into a large bowl. Add the chopped plum tomatoes, 3½ tablespoons of sherry vinegar, 5 tablespoons of olive oil, and a generous sprinkle of salt and pepper.

03 Get your hands stuck in and crush everything into a pulp. Once it is broken down, get the blender involved.

04 Blend until smooth, and then ladle the gazpacho into a pitcher.

05 Serve in glasses with lots of ice, a drizzle of good olive oil on top at the end, and a bit of extra pepper. Enjoy!

ONE-POT VEGGIE SOUPS (4 WAYS)

SERVES 4

 ꞏꞏꞏ|ꞏ|ꞏ||ꞏ|ꞏ||ꞏ||||ꞏ|ꞏꞏ|ꞏ|ꞏ|

Mary Clark
Take Me I'm Yours

ALL FOUR OF THESE
SOUP OPTIONS ARE
RIDICULOUSLY SIMPLE.
APART FROM A BIT OF
ROASTING, THEY ARE
ALL DONE IN ONE POT.
SO MINIMAL WASHING
UP. THEY ARE GREAT FOR
FREEZING AS WELL, SO
COOK IN BATCHES AND
SAVE FOR A RAINY DAY.

CARROT & CILANTRO

INGREDIENTS

1 onion
ground coriander
10 carrots
vegetable bouillon cube
fresh cilantro
dried chili flakes
2 limes
olive oil
salt and pepper

01 Pour some olive oil into a large saucepan, add the chopped onion, and fry until soft and translucent. Add 1 teaspoon of ground coriander and fry for a minute. Season with salt and pepper.

02 Chop up your carrots roughly. Add the carrots, a bouillon cube, and 4¼ cups of boiling water to the pan and simmer for 30 minutes over medium heat (or until the carrots are fully cooked).

03 Take the soup off the heat. Add a large handful of fresh cilantro and decant the mixture into a blender. Whiz until completely smooth.

04 Add 2 teaspoons of chili flakes and the juice of a lime, and mix in. Serve with another squeeze of lime juice and some more cilantro on top.

COCONUT & TOMATO

INGREDIENTS

2 red onions
6 tomatoes
garlic
14-oz. can of coconut milk
tomato paste
olive oil
salt and pepper

01 Preheat your oven to 400°F.

02 Chop up your red onions and tomatoes roughly.

03 Prepare a garlic bulb for roasting. Cut the top off, wrap in foil, leaving the top open, pour a generous amount of olive oil over, then close the foil.

04 Place everything in a roasting pan and roast in the oven for 1 hour. The onions may need only 45 minutes (remove when cooked and starting to blacken).

05 Add the onions, tomatoes, roasted garlic flesh, coconut milk, and a tablespoon of tomato paste to a large pan. Mix and season with salt and pepper (to taste). Simmer for 10 minutes.

06 Blend with a handheld blender in the pan. Enjoy!

PETITS POIS & ROASTED GARLIC

INGREDIENTS

garlic
1 onion
fresh thyme
1 lb. 2 oz. frozen petits pois
vegetable bouillon cube
cider vinegar
fresh parsley
olive oil
salt and pepper

01 Preheat your oven to 425°F.

02 Cut the top off a garlic bulb, wrap in foil, leaving the top open, pour a generous amount of olive oil over, then close the foil. Roast in the oven for 45 minutes until soft and mellow.

03 Chop up the onion and add the leaves from 3 thyme sprigs. Fry in a little olive oil in a saucepan until soft.

04 Add the frozen petits pois, a bouillon cube, 4¼ cups of boiling water, 2 tablespoons of cider vinegar, and some salt and pepper. Wait until it boils and then reduce the heat to low, add 2 handfuls of chopped fresh parsley and let simmer for 10 minutes.

05 Squeeze the flesh out from the roasted garlic and into the pan. Take a handheld blender and blend the soup in the pan until smooth. Enjoy!

CURRIED CAULIFLOWER

INGREDIENTS

1 cauliflower
2 onions
garlic
ground coriander
ground turmeric
ground cumin
14-oz. can of coconut milk
vegetable bouillon cube
unsalted cashews
1 red chili
1 lime
olive oil
salt and pepper

01 Chop up the cauliflower, onions, and 3 garlic cloves roughly. Heat some olive oil in a pan. Add the onions to the pan and fry until soft and translucent. Add the garlic, ½ teaspoon of ground coriander, ½ teaspoon of ground turmeric, and 1 teaspoon of ground cumin and fry for 1–2 minutes to release the aromas. Season with salt and pepper.

02 Add the chopped cauliflower, coconut milk, bouillon cube, and 4¼ cups of boiling water. Stir well and bring to a boil. Once boiling, turn the heat down to low and simmer for 20 minutes (or until the cauliflower is tender and soft).

03 Blend with a handheld blender in the pan until smooth. Season with salt and pepper again.

04 Toast some cashews in a separate dry pan for a few minutes. Seed and slice the chili.

05 Serve the soup with the toasted cashews, a few slices of seeded red chili, and a squeeze of lime.

SERVES 4
45 mins

Baba Stiltz
Beirut

INGREDIENTS

cumin seeds
mustard seeds
2 red chilies
2 white onions
garlic
fresh ginger
2 x 14-oz. cans of green
jackfruit pieces
14 oz. (2¼ cups) basmati rice
ground coriander
ground turmeric
tomato paste
17 fl. oz. jar (about 2 cups) of
strained tomatoes
coconut cream
fresh cilantro
olive oil

**THE MEATIEST VEGAN
CURRY YOU'LL EVER
MUNCH. SIMPLE AS THAT.**

MIGHTY JACKFRUIT CURRY [VG]

01 Add a splash of olive oil to a frying pan or skillet and add 1 teaspoon of cumin seeds and the same of mustard seeds, pan-frying for a minute to release the aroma. Add the chopped and seeded red chilies, chopped onions, 5 chopped garlic cloves, and a chopped 1-inch piece of ginger. Cook until the onions are soft and translucent.

02 Drain and rinse your jackfruit (to remove as much salt as possible).

03 Put the rice on to cook in a separate pan and cook according to the package instructions. Drain.

04 Add 1½ teaspoons of ground coriander, 1 teaspoon of ground turmeric, 2 tablespoons of tomato paste, and the jackfruit to the onions. Mix together, pour in the strained tomatoes, cover your pan, and cook for 10 minutes.

05 Uncover and shred the jackfruit a bit and allow the sauce to thicken. Add 2 tablespoons of coconut cream and a little water if necessary. Mix everything together.

06 Bubble the curry down until it is nice and thick. Scatter over a handful of chopped cilantro. Serve on a bed of steaming rice.

INGREDIENTS

2 onions
garlic
1 carrot
1 cauliflower
cinnamon stick
cardamom pods
cumin seeds
bay leaves
ground turmeric
basmati rice
vegan margarine
vegetable oil
salt and pepper

AHHHHH PILAF. THOSE AROMATIC SMELLS. THE BEAUTY OF THIS RECIPE IS THAT IT IS ALL IN ONE POT. YOU CAN ADD WHATEVER VEGGIES YOU LIKE TO IT, SO IF YOU'VE GOT ANY LEFTOVER PRODUCE, THROW IT IN!

FRAGRANT VEGGIE PILAF [VG]

01 Finely chop your onions and 2 garlic cloves, then fry them over low heat with a splash of vegetable oil until the onions are soft and translucent.

02 Chop the carrot into small cubes. Break up the cauliflower into little florets and chop up finely. Add both to the pan and fry for 2 minutes.

03 Add your spices—1 cinnamon stick, 2 crushed cardamom pods, 1 teaspoon of cumin seeds, 3 bay leaves, and 1 teaspoon of ground turmeric. Season with salt and pepper. Stir well.

04 Meanwhile, rinse 1¾ cups of basmati rice and then add to the pan with 3 cups of water. Mix well, then cook on low heat for 20 minutes or so until the rice is cooked and there is no liquid left in the pan.

05 Fluff up your rice, remove the cinnamon stick, cardamom pods, and bay leaves (if desired), and add a heaped tablespoon of vegan margarine before serving.

CREAMY VEGAN KORMA [★] [VG]

SERVES 4
1 hr

Sly5thAve
Get Free

INGREDIENTS

1 eggplant
1 butternut squash
1 onion
fresh ginger
garlic
sesame oil
garam masala
dried chili flakes
tomato paste
14 oz. (2¼ cups) basmati rice
12 oz. (1½ cups) dairy-free coconut yogurt (we use The Coconut Collaborative)
fresh cilantro
unsalted cashews
1 lime
olive oil
salt and pepper

CREAMY, COCONUTTY, SOOTHING. WHAT MORE COULD YOU WANT FROM A CURRY? THE CASHEWS BRING THE CRUNCH.

01 Preheat your oven to 400°F.

02 Cube the eggplant and seed and peel the butternut squash. Add to a baking sheet. Drizzle with olive oil, season with salt and pepper and roast in the oven for 35 minutes.

03 Meanwhile, get your korma on. Finely chop the onion and grate a thumb-size piece of ginger and 2 garlic cloves. Heat 1½ tablespoons of sesame oil in a large frying pan or skillet and add the onion, ginger, and garlic. Fry until soft, then add 2 teaspoons of garam masala, a teaspoon of chili flakes, and 2 tablespoons of tomato paste. Stir everything together, and then add scant 1 cup of water.

04 In the meantime, put your basmati rice on to cook in a separate pan and cook according to the package instructions.

05 Add the "yogurt" to the korma and stir it in. Add your roasted vegetables, with a large handful of chopped cilantro (reserve some to garnish), ½ cup cashews, and the juice of a lime, and stir in.

06 Serve the korma over the steaming hot rice with the remaining chopped cilantro scattered on top.

SILKY LEEK RISOTTO

SERVES 4
45 mins

Dope Lemon
Marinade

INGREDIENTS

2 white onions
3 large leeks
10½ oz. (1½ cups) arborio rice
¾ cup white wine
1 vegetarian bouillon cube
pecorino
Parmesan
olive oil
salt and pepper

THE FINEST LITTLE RIZZY THIS SIDE OF THE ATLANTIC. MAKE SURE YOU COOK THE LEEKS UNTIL THEY ARE SILKY AND SMOOTH—LOW AND SLOW, PAPI.

01 Wash and dice your onions and leeks.

02 Heat a frying pan or skillet with a splash of olive oil over medium heat. Add your onions and leeks, cooking until they are soft and translucent. Season with salt and pepper.

03 Take one-quarter of the mixture out, cover to keep warm and put to the side and salt generously.

04 Pour the arborio rice into the pan. Mix for a minute, so that the rice becomes slightly translucent.

05 Wine time! Pour in the wine and mix while it slowly evaporates.

06 Mix your veggie bouillon cube with 3 cups of boiling water.

07 Ladle in the stock, mix the risotto continuously while cooking over medium–low heat, and then wait until the stock has been absorbed.

08 Once it has dried up, add another ladle of stock. Continue stirring. Repeat until the rice is al dente. Keep ladling in the stock if needs be.

09 Add half a grated block of pecorino and half a grated block of Parmesan, and mix thoroughly.

10 Take the pan off the heat and serve each portion with some of the reserved salted leek and onion mixture and grated cheese on top!

SERVES 4
55 mins

Blend Crafters
The Sh*t

INGREDIENTS

2 butternut squash
vegetable bouillon cube
garlic
2¾ cups dried orzo pasta
fresh basil
goat cheese
Parmesan
olive oil
salt and pepper

THE OOZIEST ORZO ABOUT—THE PERFECT AUTUMN WARMER. THE BASIL AND THE GOAT CHEESE REALLY FRESHEN THE DISH UP, SO DON'T SKIP EITHER OF THEM. ALSO, WHEN YOU FIRST ROAST YOUR BUTTERNUT SQUASH, YOU DON'T WANT IT TO GET BROWN AND CHARRED. JUST SOFT. SO KEEP AN EYE ON IT.

OOZY BUTTERNUT ORZO [★]

01 Preheat your oven to 400°F.

02 Seed, peel, and cut your butternut squash into cubes, and place on a baking sheet. Drizzle with olive oil and season with salt and pepper. Roast in the oven for 30 minutes or until soft.

03 Remove the squash (when it's soft) from the oven. Place three-quarters in a blender. Place the remainder back in the oven until brown and caramelized, then remove and set aside.

04 Add a vegetable bouillon cube and scant 2½ cups of water into the blender. Whiz. You want quite a loose puree consistency.

05 Place a large frying pan or skillet over the heat. Add 1 chopped garlic clove with a splash of olive oil. Once softened, pour in the squash puree. Mix it about, and then add the orzo.

06 Keep mixing the orzo about, and pouring in splashes of water until the orzo has cooked through and resembles a loose, oozy risotto. At this point, add your remaining caramelized squash, and a handful of chopped basil (leave some whole leaves to garnish). Mix it all together and turn off the heat.

07 Add large dollops of goat cheese on top of the orzo, sprinkle over some grated Parmesan, scatter on the reserved whole basil leaves, and serve with a final drizzle of olive oil. Enjoy!

SERVES 4

1 hr 20 mins

The War on Drugs
Red Eyes

INGREDIENTS

2 onions
garlic
ground cumin
ground cinnamon
harissa
3 eggplants
14-oz. can of plum tomatoes
14-oz. can of chickpeas
14 oz. (2⅓ cups) couscous
1 lemon
pitted dates
fresh cilantro
olive oil
salt and pepper

A DELICIOUS VEGAN TAGINE. SLOW COOKING IS THE KEY HERE. MAKE SURE YOU ADD THE SPICES AT THE START SO THEY RELEASE THEIR OILS. BIG UP THE TAGINE.

CHICKPEA, EGGPLANT & DATE TAGINE [VG]

01 Chop the onions roughly, and finely chop 2 garlic cloves. Place a large frying pan or skillet over medium heat and add a splash of olive oil. Add your spices—1½ teaspoons of ground cumin, 1 teaspoon of ground cinnamon, and 3 teaspoons of harissa—and cook until the onions start to look translucent.

02 Chop your eggplants into large chunks and add to the pan. Keep cooking for another 10 minutes, stirring continuously to get all the spices and flavors into the eggplant.

03 Next, add the tomatoes and chickpeas with their water. Season with salt and pepper, give it a good stir, then place the lid on and simmer for 1 hour, or until thick and the eggplant is cooked through.

04 With a few minutes to go, cook the couscous according to the package instructions, then add a squeeze of lemon juice.

05 Stir a handful of pitted dates into the tagine. Serve the tagine on top of the couscous and garnish with a squeeze of lemon and a scattering of cilantro leaves.

SERVES 4
1 hr

Subculture Sage
Happy Like the Sunking

INGREDIENTS

1 large cauliflower
ground cumin
ground coriander
ground turmeric
garlic
1 lemon
14 oz. (1¾ cups) dairy-free
coconut yogurt
1 cucumber
fresh mint
7 oz. (about 1¼ cups) fresh
pomegranate seeds, and extra
for garnish
14 oz. (2⅓ cups) couscous
raisins
fresh parsley
olive oil
salt and pepper

A REAL VEGAN
SHOWSTOPPER. THE
CAULIFLOWER IS SO
GOOD. TRY AND FIND A
NICE BIG CAULIFLOWER
FOR THIS—PEOPLE ARE
GOING TO BE FIGHTING
OVER IT.

BAKED SPICED CAULIFLOWER WITH TZATZIKI [VG]

01 Preheat your oven to 425°F.

02 Trim the base of your large cauliflower and remove any green leaves.

03 In a bowl, combine 2 teaspoons of ground cumin, 1 teaspoon of ground coriander, and ½ teaspoon of ground turmeric. Add a crushed garlic clove and some salt and pepper. Pour in 2 tablespoons of olive oil. Mix together well until you have a thick paste.

04 Spread the paste over the cauliflower and place on a baking sheet, then roast in the oven until the surface is dry—around 45 minutes.

05 Meanwhile, it's tzatziki time. Zest 1 lemon and squeeze its juices into a separate bowl with half the coconut yogurt.

06 Finely grate the cucumber (squeeze the gratings to remove excess moisture) and add to the lemon yogurt with a handful of chopped mint and 3½ oz. of the pomegranate seeds. Season with salt and pepper and set aside.

07 Couscous time. Add the couscous to a heatproof bowl. Cover with boiling water so there is about 1 inch of water on top of the couscous. Allow it to absorb the water for 5 minutes, and then fluff it up with a fork. Add 1 cup of raisins, a handful of chopped parsley, the remaining 3½ oz. of pomegranate seeds, salt, pepper, and a splash of olive oil. Mix together.

08 When cooked, let the cauliflower cool and then serve in thick slices with a spoonful of your homemade tzatziki and your couscous (with a sprinkling of extra pomegranate seeds on top). Garnish with some extra torn mint and parsley.

5

FLASHY MOB

CAPONATA PARMIGIANA

SERVES 4

2 hrs

St. Germain

Rose Rouge

INGREDIENTS

3 large eggplants
all-purpose flour
1 red onion
fresh parsley
capers
pitted Kalamata olives
red wine vinegar
3 x 14-oz. cans of plum tomatoes
3 large mozzarella balls
Parmesan
olive oil
salt and pepper

A TWIST ON AN ITALIAN CLASSIC THAT IS EVEN BETTER COLD THE NEXT DAY. DON'T FORGET TO SALT YOUR EGGPLANTS TO REMOVE THE BITTER TASTE AND DRAW OUT EXCESS WATER.

01 Preheat your oven to 350°F.

02 Cut the eggplants lengthwise into ¼–½-inch strips. Place them in a bowl and sprinkle generously with salt. After 30 minutes, pour the excess water out of the bowl and brush off any excess salt. Coat the eggplant slices with flour.

03 Pour some olive oil into a frying pan or skillet over medium heat and fry the eggplants until lightly browned on each side. Remove from the pan and set aside.

04 Chop the onion and sauté in the pan with a little more olive oil, if necessary. Allow the onion to soften until translucent and then add a handful of chopped parsley stalks, 2 tablespoons each of capers and olives, and 4 tablespoons of red wine vinegar. Stir well and, once the vinegar has evaporated, add the tomatoes. Break them up and leave the sauce to simmer for 6–7 minutes, until very thick. Add some chopped parsley leaves, then season with salt and pepper and remove from the heat.

05 Spoon some of the tomato sauce into a baking dish. Layer up with eggplant, more tomato sauce, and sliced mozzarella. Keep repeating until the dish is full. Finish off with a layer of mozzarella and grated Parmesan. Drizzle over some olive oil and season with salt and pepper.

06 Place the dish in the oven and bake for 35 minutes, then remove and place it under a preheated hot broiler until the cheese is golden and bubbling.

07 Leave for at least 30 minutes to set before serving. Then slice up the parmigiana and tuck in!

INGREDIENTS

4 eggplants
red miso paste
maple syrup
mirin
14 oz. (2¼ cups) jasmine rice
toasted sesame oil
sesame seeds

**MAKE SURE YOU
FOLLOW THE SOAKING
INSTRUCTIONS IN THIS
RECIPE—IT IS KEY TO
MAKING SURE YOU
GET THE SWEETEST,
SQUIDGIEST EGGPLANT.**

MISO-GLAZED STICKY EGGPLANTS WITH SESAME RICE [VG]

01 Preheat your oven to 480°F.

02 Peel and cut the eggplants into 1-inch thick wedges. Soak in cold water for 5–10 minutes to remove tannins (which make eggplants taste bitter). The water you pour out will be brown.

03 Make the sauce by mixing 5½ oz. miso paste, 5½ oz. maple syrup, and 5 tablespoons of mirin in a bowl. Set aside.

04 Coat the bottom of a baking dish in oil. Pat the eggplants dry with paper towels and place in the baking dish. Arrange them so that there are no overlaps and place the dish in the oven.

05 Meanwhile, cook the jasmine rice according to the package instructions. Add a teaspoon of sesame oil to the cooked (drained) rice.

06 Once the eggplants are nearly done (check if a fork can go in easily), add most of the sauce, toss to mix, and place back in the oven. Make sure the sauce doesn't burn! Once almost ready, brush the eggplants with the leftover sauce for added stickiness.

07 Serve on a bed of rice with sesame seeds scattered on top.

INGREDIENTS

vegetable bouillon cube
1 lb. 2 oz. (3¼ cups) fine
cornmeal
6 portobello mushrooms
1 red onion
garlic
balsamic vinegar
butter
Parmesan
fresh parsley
olive oil

IF I HAD A DOLLAR FOR
EVERY TIME I'VE BEEN
TOLD THAT POLENTA
IS BORING I'D BE A
MILLIONAIRE. WELL, THIS
IS THE DISH TO PROVE THE
POLENTA HATERS WRONG.
RICH. CREAMY. CHEESY.
IT HAS IT ALL.

CREAMY POLENTA WITH PORTOBELLO MUSHROOMS

01 Add the bouillon cube to 8½ cups of water in a pan. Bring to a boil, add the cornmeal, and whisk to prevent lumps. Cook according to the package instructions.

02 Reduce the heat to medium–low so the polenta bubbles (but doesn't go everywhere), making sure to stir every few minutes so it doesn't catch or burn. Cook for about 30 minutes until it thickens.

03 Meanwhile, slice up your mushrooms, chop up the onion, and dice 2 garlic cloves.

04 Heat a frying pan or skillet with some olive oil, add the onion, and when it starts to look translucent, add the garlic. When both are soft, add your mushrooms and a splash of balsamic vinegar.

05 When the polenta is cooked, add a big pat of butter and a handful of grated cheese, and mix well so that it all melts.

06 Back to the mushrooms. When the balsamic is slightly sticky and the mushrooms are plump and soft, serve the mushrooms on top of the creamy polenta. Garnish with chopped parsley and sprinkle with some extra Parmesan.

SHAHI SPINACH PANEER

SERVES 4
40 mins

Bastien Keb
Fit Rare

INGREDIENTS

unsalted cashews
14 oz. (2¼ cups) basmati rice
1 onion
fresh ginger
garlic
chili powder
garam masala
ground turmeric
7 oz. tomato paste
7 oz. paneer cheese
heavy cream
fresh spinach
fresh cilantro
olive oil
salt and pepper

A PUNJABI SPECIAL FOR UNDER 20 BUCKS. DITCH THE TAKEOUT AND WHIP UP THIS INSTEAD. ONE NOTE OF CAUTION: BE CAREFUL WHEN HANDLING THE TURMERIC, IT STAINS EVERYTHING!

01 Soak a handful of cashews in warm water for at least 15 minutes while preparing the other ingredients.

02 Cook the rice, following the package instructions. Drain.

03 Meanwhile, dice the onion and a 1-inch piece of ginger. Finely chop 4 garlic cloves. Place them all into a frying pan or skillet with a drizzle of olive oil and sauté until soft. Add salt, pepper, ½ teaspoon of chili powder, ½ teaspoon of garam masala, and ½ teaspoon of ground turmeric.

04 Let simmer until the onion gets soft and translucent. Turn off the heat and let cool slightly.

05 After the cashews have been soaked and onion cooked, add them both to a blender and whiz to make a smooth paste.

06 Heat some olive oil in a frying pan or skillet, then add the paste. Cook on low until most of the moisture evaporates, then add the tomato paste.

07 Stir well and cook until the oil starts to ooze out from the sides. Stir frequently to make sure that it is not sticking to the bottom of the pan.

08 Add another ½ teaspoon of garam masala and mix well. Cube the paneer, add to the pan, mix well, and allow to simmer for 2 minutes.

09 Add 4 tablespoons of heavy cream and mix in. Add some spinach and let cook for a few more minutes.

10 Serve on a bed of rice and garnish with fresh cilantro leaves.

SERVES 4
2 hrs

Natty Reeves
Solace

INGREDIENTS

1 large butternut squash
2 sweet potatoes
2 red bell peppers
1 onion
garlic
14 oz. fresh spinach
7-oz. block of feta cheese
1 lemon

SQUASH, SPINACH & RED PEPPER PIE

01 Preheat your oven to 350°F.

02 Seed, peel, and cube the squash and sweet potatoes. Put in a baking dish, season with salt and pepper, and drizzle with olive oil. Cook for 50 minutes, or until cooked through.

03 At the same time, put the whole red peppers on a baking sheet and roast in the oven for 40 minutes.

04 Meanwhile, finely chop the onion and 2 garlic cloves. Add to a frying pan or skillet with a splash of olive oil. Fry until the onion is soft, then add your spinach. Wilt the spinach down and season with salt and pepper.

05 Transfer the spinach mixture to a strainer. Squeeze with a wooden spoon to get rid of excess moisture. Add the spinach to a mixing bowl and crumble in half of the feta and the zest of a lemon. Set to one side.

9 oz. (1 cup) ricotta cheese
4 eggs
9 oz. phyllo pastry
sesame seeds
olive oil
salt and pepper

THIS BANGING VEGGIE PIE IS WARMING, FILLING, AND THE SESAME SEEDS PERFECT THE CRUNCHY TOP!

06 Remove the red peppers from the oven, put them in a bowl, cover with plastic wrap, and let cool. Peel off the skins, remove the seeds, and cut into quarters.

07 Remove the potatoes and squash from the oven and roughly mash together in a second mixing bowl. Add the remaining feta, the ricotta, and the beaten eggs. Season with salt and pepper, and mix everything together. Keep the oven on.

08 Pie time. Brush a 2-lb. loaf pan or other pie dish with olive oil. Add a layer of phyllo pastry. Brush with olive oil. Then repeat with four more layers of phyllo.

09 Put the spinach mixture on the bottom, followed by the potato and squash mixture. Top it with the roasted red peppers and fold the edges of the pastry over the top. Add 3–4 crumpled sheets of phyllo on the top for extra crunch. Brush well with olive oil and sprinkle with sesame seeds.

10 Bake the pie in the still-hot oven for 50 minutes, or until golden brown.

11 Slice the pie and tuck in!

THE N'CASCIATA

SERVES 4
1 hr 10 mins

Franc Moody
Dopamine

INGREDIENTS

5 eggplants
1 red onion
garlic
fresh parsley
capers
red wine vinegar
pitted Kalamata olives
14-oz. can of plum tomatoes
1 lb. 2 oz. (about 6 cups) dried
rigatoni pasta
Parmesan
olive oil

A SERIOUSLY IMPRESSIVE DISH. AN EGGPLANT AND PASTA CAKE—BASICALLY YOU CAN USE A CIRCULAR CAKE PAN OR A SQUARE BAKING DISH. JUST MAKE SURE THE SIDES ARE HIGH ENOUGH.

01 Preheat your oven to 400°F.

02 Cut 3 of your eggplants into long, thin slices. Grill each slice (DON'T ADD OIL!) on a griddle (ridged stovetop) pan until charred and soft. If you don't have a griddle, use a frying pan or skillet. Set the eggplant slices to one side.

03 Time to make the sauce! Dice the remaining eggplants into ¾-inch chunks. Dice the red onion and grate a garlic clove.

04 Add the diced eggplant to a frying pan or skillet, but again, don't add any oil. Cook until the eggplant is evenly browned.

05 At this point, add a splash of olive oil, the diced onion, grated garlic, and a large handful of chopped parsley and cook for another couple of minutes.

06 Add 2 tablespoons of capers, 3 tablespoons of red wine vinegar, and a handful of pitted Kalamata olives to the pan and cook for another minute.

07 Add the plum tomatoes and crush with a wooden spoon. Simmer for 10 minutes.

08 While the sauce is simmering away, boil the rigatoni (as per the package instructions) until al dente, then drain and add it to the sauce with a splash of the pasta water. Stir to combine.

09 Find a deep baking dish (preferably metal). Line it with most of your sliced eggplants. First line the bottom, making sure all the sides overlap. Then place them around the edges until all sides are covered.

10 Spoon in your rigatoni mixture, and then place the remaining eggplant slices over the top so the pasta filling is covered. Grate over some Parmesan, and then cover with foil. Bake in the preheated oven for 20 minutes.

11 Remove the dish from the oven and take off the foil. Place the dish back in the oven for 4 minutes so the Parmesan melts. Remove from the oven.

12 Place a plate on top of the dish. Flip it, then ease the pan off the pasta cake. Grate some Parmesan over the top. Slice it up and tuck in!

VEGGIE MOUSSAKA

SERVES 4
50 mins

Khruangbin
Two Fish and an Elephant

INGREDIENTS

2 eggplants
7-oz. block of feta cheese
9 oz. (1 cup) ricotta cheese
1 lemon
1 egg
2 onions
garlic
ground cinnamon
dried oregano
fresh parsley
2 x 14-oz. cans of chopped
tomatoes
dried red lentils
olive oil
salt and pepper

LEAVE THE DISH TO SET FOR 30 MINUTES SO THAT IT'S EASY TO SERVE UP! BAKING THE EGGPLANT SLICES BEFOREHAND ENSURES THEY ARE NICE AND SOFT. THIS ONE IS AN ABSOLUTE BELTER SERVED COLD THE NEXT DAY.

01 Preheat your oven to 400°F.

02 Finely slice the eggplants lengthwise. Place on a baking sheet, season generously with salt and pepper, then bake in the oven for 15 minutes. Remove and set aside (keep hot).

03 Meanwhile, in a bowl, add the crumbled block of feta, the ricotta, the zest of a lemon, and the egg, then season with salt, pepper, and a splash of olive oil. Mix everything together and set aside for later.

04 Finely chop your onions and 2 garlic cloves. Fry in a large saucepan with a little olive oil until soft, then add 1 teaspoon of ground cinnamon and 2 teaspoons of dried oregano. Season with salt and pepper, and then add a large handful of chopped parsley.

05 Mix together, then add your canned tomatoes and 2½ cups of water.

06 Wash 2 cups of red lentils, then pour them into the sauce. Mix, and then cook over medium heat for 15–20 minutes until the lentils have cooked through and the sauce has thickened. Remove from the heat.

07 Layering time. Into a baking dish, spoon in half of your lentil mixture, then cover it with half of your cooked eggplant slices. Cover the eggplant with the other half of the lentil mix, and then cover this with your remaining eggplants. Cover it all with your feta and ricotta mix, then place under a preheated hot broiler for 10 minutes, or until the feta and ricotta mix starts to get little burn marks over it.

08 Remove from the broiler, let rest for 30 minutes, then slice up and enjoy!

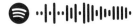
INGREDIENTS

1 red bell pepper
1 small butternut squash
2 sweet potatoes
14 oz. (2¼ cups) basmati rice
2 red onions
garlic
tomato paste
1 red chili
fresh parsley
paprika
14-oz. can of black beans
2 x 14-oz. cans of chopped tomatoes
bittersweet chocolate
brown sugar
lemon
olive oil
salt and pepper

A BRAZILIAN CLASSIC WITH A VEGGIE TWIST. ADDING CHOCOLATE BRINGS THE RICHNESS HERE, AND THERE SHOULD BE SOME LEFT OVER FOR NIBBLING AT THE END. BUT CHECK THAT IT IS VEGAN, AS SOME BRANDS CONTAIN MILK.

ROASTED VEGETABLE FEIJOADA [VG]

01 Preheat your oven to 400°F.

02 Seed and chop up the red pepper. Peel, seed, and chop the butternut squash. Scrub, peel, and chop the sweet potatoes. Add all these to a roasting pan and roast in the oven for 40 minutes.

03 Meanwhile, cook the rice according to the package instructions. Drain.

04 Dice the red onions and 2 garlic cloves. Gently fry the onions, garlic, 1 tablespoon of tomato paste, and the chopped red chili (seeded) with a little olive oil for 5 minutes. Chop up a handful of parsley stalks and add with 1 teaspoon of paprika, then fry for another minute. Season generously with salt and pepper.

05 Drain and rinse your beans, then add them to the mix along with the tomatoes. Add 2¼ oz. of bittersweet chocolate and a heaped tablespoon of brown sugar. Mix well and allow to simmer and bubble down.

06 Add the roasted veggies to the mix. Stir them in and cook for another 10 minutes so the vegetables absorb all the flavor.

07 Serve on a bed of rice, squeeze lots of lemon juice on top, and add the rest of the roughly chopped parsley leaves for garnish.

INGREDIENTS

1 onion
garlic
sugar
2 x 14-oz. cans of chopped tomatoes
pitted Kalamata olives
4 fennel bulbs
dried breadcrumbs
7 oz. Gouda cheese
olive oil
salt and pepper

THE FENNEL BECOMES ALL UNCTUOUS WHEN YOU SLOW COOK IT. MAKE SURE THE BREADCRUMBS ARE GOLDEN AND CRUNCHY BEFORE SERVING. MOZZARELLA WOULD WORK WELL IN THIS BAKE, TOO.

FENNEL & TOMATO TRAYBAKE WITH GOUDA & BREADCRUMB TOPPING

01 Preheat your oven to 350°F.

02 Finely chop the onion and 3 garlic cloves and fry with a splash of olive oil until the onion is soft and translucent. Add 2 teaspoons of sugar. Once it has dissolved, add your tomatoes and allow to cook over low heat for 20 minutes so that it bubbles down into a lovely, rich sauce.

03 Take the sauce off the heat. Chop a handful of Kalamata olives in half and add to the sauce.

04 Heat some olive oil in another saucepan. Meanwhile, chop the fennel bulbs into large chunks, then add to the saucepan, cover, and stew over low heat for 15 minutes. Add your tomato sauce and season with salt and pepper. Simmer until the sauce is thick. Pour into a baking dish.

05 Sprinkle the dish with the breadcrumbs, drizzle generously with olive oil, and place slices of Gouda on top. Bake in the oven for 20 minutes until the breadcrumbs and cheese are golden.

06 Remove from the oven, spoon it out on to plates, and enjoy!

INGREDIENTS

4 sweet potatoes
10½ oz. (1¾ cups) quinoa
7 oz. kale
1 lemon
tahini
honey
chipotle chili paste
slivered almonds
fresh pomegranate seeds
olive oil
salt and pepper

A GREAT SUMMER DISH— THE SWEET POTATOES COOK PERFECTLY IN THE COALS OF THE BBQ. THE TAHINI DRESSING IS SO CREAMY, YOU WON'T BELIEVE IT'S VEGGIE.

LOADED BBQ SWEET POTATOES WITH TAHINI DRESSING

01 Set up the barbecue and fire up the coals.

02 Wash the sweet potatoes, rub with a little olive oil and salt, then double wrap in foil. When the coals are glowing red, put the wrapped potatoes directly on top of them for 15 minutes, turn, and cook for another 15 minutes.

03 While these are cooking, put a pan of water on to boil. When bubbling, add the quinoa. Cook for 15 minutes.

04 Stem the kale leaves and thinly slice. Add to a large bowl, add some olive oil, and massage the leaves for a minute (it makes them more tender).

05 Add the juice of a lemon, 2 tablespoons of tahini, a generous tablespoon of honey, and 2 tablespoons of chipotle paste into the bowl. Season with salt and pepper, then mix thoroughly.

06 Remove a potato and check if it's cooked thoroughly. Take the quinoa off the heat, drain, and toss with your kale and tahini dressing. Split the potatoes open and top with the dressed quinoa and kale.

07 Quickly toast the slivered almonds in a dry frying pan or skillet, then top the potatoes with them. Shake a handful of pomegranate seeds on top. Enjoy!

FAKEOUT MOB

6

INGREDIENTS

3 red onions
cumin seeds
garam masala
ground coriander
fresh ginger
fresh cilantro
baking powder
chickpea (gram) flour
5½ oz. (¾ cup) dairy-free
coconut yogurt
1 cucumber
fresh mint
4 brioche buns
mango chutney
vegetable oil
salt and pepper

THESE BHAJI BURGERS
ARE THE ONE. THE FRESH
HOMEMADE COCONUT
RAITA MAKES THEM!
SWITCH OUT THE BRIOCHE
BUNS FOR REGULAR
SEEDED BUNS TO KEEP
IT SUITABLE FOR
THE VEGANS!

BIG BOY BHAJI BURGERS [★]

01 Finely slice the red onions. Add them to a mixing bowl with 2 teaspoons of cumin seeds, 2 teaspoons of garam masala, and 2 teaspoons of ground coriander. Add a teaspoon of grated ginger, a tablespoon of chopped cilantro stalks, a teaspoon of baking powder, 4 tablespoons of chickpea flour, and 6 tablespoons of water. Mix everything together until it resembles a chunky, oniony batter. Set to one side.

02 Make your raita. Add the coconut yogurt to a separate bowl. Add a large handful of grated cucumber (squeeze the gratings to get rid of excess water), a handful each of chopped mint and cilantro leaves, and some salt and pepper. Mix well.

03 Heat some vegetable oil in a frying pan or skillet. Add a tablespoon of your bhaji batter. Flatten it out and fry for 2–3 minutes on each side until deep golden brown. Cook two bhajis per burger.

04 Cut your brioche buns in half and put them under the preheated hot broiler to toast up.

05 Assembly time. Add a big dollop of raita to each bun. Then add a bhaji. Then more raita, then another bhaji. Top with a big dollop of mango chutney and some mint leaves. Place the lids on top. Take a big bite and enjoy!

INGREDIENTS

1 cauliflower
1 head of broccoli
all-purpose flour
2 eggs
dried breadcrumbs
1 cucumber
7 oz. radishes
1 lime
3 Little Gem lettuces
fresh cilantro
mayonnaise
sriracha sauce
1 avocado
olive oil
salt and pepper

YOU WANT THE BROCCOLI AND THE CAULIFLOWER FLORETS TO BE PERFECT BITE-SIZE PIECES, SO BEAR THAT IN MIND WHILE PREPPING. LEAVE THE CAULIFLOWER IN THE OVEN UNTIL PERFECTLY BROWN AND CRUNCHY.

BANG BANG CAULIFLOWER SALAD BOWLS

01 Preheat your oven to 350°F.

02 Break the cauliflower and broccoli into florets.

03 Get three bowls out. Add some flour to one, the beaten eggs to another, and breadcrumbs to the last.

04 Line a baking sheet with parchment paper. Dip the cauliflower and broccoli florets into the flour, the eggs, and the breadcrumbs, in that order. Season the veggies with salt, add to the lined sheet, and drizzle with olive oil, and then put the sheet in the oven for 30 minutes until golden and crunchy.

05 Meanwhile, finely chop your cucumber and the radishes. Add to a bowl with the juice of half a lime, the chopped lettuces, 3 tablespoons of olive oil, a handful of cilantro leaves, and salt and pepper. Mix together and set aside.

06 Into a bowl add 6 tablespoons of mayo, 2 tablespoons of sriracha, and the juice of half a lime. Mix everything together.

07 Serving time. Add some of the zingy radish salad to each bowl. Top with bang bang veggies, some avocado slices, a big dollop of sriracha mayo, and some fresh cilantro leaves. Enjoy!

BLACK PEPPER TOFU [★]

SERVES 4
20 mins

Tinariwen
Chaghaybou

INGREDIENTS

1¼ lb. tofu
cornstarch
14 oz. (2¼ cups) basmati rice
butter
1 white onion
garlic
fresh ginger
crushed black peppercorns
white sugar
light soy sauce
dark soy sauce
1 red chili
4 scallions
vegetable oil

01 Chop the tofu into cubes. Coat in cornstarch.

02 Add some vegetable oil to a wok. Stir-fry the tofu until browned and remove from the wok.

03 Put the rice on to cook (follow the package instructions). Drain.

04 Clean the wok and place over medium heat. Add a splash of vegetable oil. Add 4 tablespoons of butter, along with the chopped onion, 2 finely chopped garlic cloves, and a large piece of fresh ginger. Stir-fry until everything is soft. At this point, add 2 tablespoons of crushed black peppercorns and 2 tablespoons of white sugar. Stir them in. Once the sugar has dissolved, add 5 tablespoons each of light and dark soy sauces.

05 Stir it all together, and then add the chopped and seeded red chili and 3 chopped scallions. Stir, and then re-add your tofu. Stir it in, add another tablespoon of butter, allowing it to melt, then remove the wok from the heat.

06 Serve the tofu on top of a mound of steaming rice, garnish with the remaining chopped scallion and extra chili, and enjoy!

SUCH A DELICIOUS DISH. AND A GREAT WAY TO USE UP ANY LEFTOVER BLACK PEPPER! TASTE THE TOFU AT THE END. IF IT'S TOO SUGARY, ADD A BIT MORE PEPPER. IF IT'S TOO PEPPERY, ADD A BIT MORE SUGAR. GET THAT BALANCE JUST RIGHT.

QUESADILLAS (3 WAYS)

SERVES 4
15–40 mins

An Der Beat
Knuf!

MAKE IT VEGAN BY
SUBSTITUTING THE
CREAM CHEESE FOR A
VEGAN CREAM CHEESE
ALTERNATIVE!

SPINACH & ARTICHOKE QUESADILLAS

INGREDIENTS

garlic
marinated artichoke hearts
baby spinach
6 oz. (¾ cup) cream cheese
4 large flour tortillas
olive oil
salt and pepper

01 Heat some olive oil in a frying pan or skillet. Chop up 2 garlic cloves and add to the pan, sautéing for 1 minute.

02 Cut up the artichoke hearts and add to the pan along with 3 large handfuls of baby spinach. Stir to combine and cook until the spinach begins to wilt.

03 Add the cream cheese and some salt and pepper to the pan, and stir to combine. Heat all the way through and then put to the side.

04 Place a separate nonstick pan on the stovetop over medium-high heat. Put one tortilla in the pan and fill with a quarter of the artichoke mixture and another half handful of baby spinach—spread only on one half of the tortilla.

05 Fold the tortilla in half, cook until the bottom is brown (around 2 minutes), then flip over to brown the other side for another couple of minutes. Remove to a plate.

06 Repeat for the remaining tortillas.

07 Slice each tortilla in half and serve!

CHEESY CORN & SMASHED AVOCADO QUESADILLAS

INGREDIENTS

garlic
2 avocados
Cheddar cheese
4 large flour tortillas
9¼ oz. (1¾ cups) drained
canned corn kernals
olive oil

01 Dice 5 garlic cloves. Heat a splash of olive oil in a frying pan or skillet and sauté the garlic until soft.

02 Scoop out the avocado flesh and mash in a bowl

03 Grate your Cheddar.

04 Place a nonstick frying pan or skillet on the stovetop over medium-high heat. Put one tortilla in the pan and fill with a quarter of the cooked garlic, smashed avocado, and corn—spread only on one half of the tortilla. Sprinkle over some grated cheese.

05 Fold the tortilla in half, cook until the bottom is brown (around 2 minutes), then flip over to brown the other side for another couple of minutes. Remove to a plate.

06 Repeat for the remaining tortillas. Slice each tortilla in half and serve!

SWEET POTATO, BLACK BEAN & CARAMELIZED ONION QUESADILLAS [VG]

INGREDIENTS

3 red onions
2 sweet potatoes
balsamic vinegar
14-oz. can of black beans
4 large flour tortillas
dried chili flakes
olive oil

01 Slice the onions into long strips.

02 Heat some olive oil in a frying pan or skillet over medium heat until the oil is hot. Add the onions and some water. Cook for 30 minutes, stirring regularly, until the onions are caramelized. Add a little more water if the onions start sticking to the bottom of the pan or crisping.

03 Meanwhile, scrub and then cook the sweet potatoes in a microwave or oven.

04 When the onions are caramelized, turn off the heat and add some balsamic vinegar, mixing it thoroughly.

05 Drain and rinse the can of black beans and set aside.

06 Place a nonstick frying pan or skillet on the stovetop over medium–high heat. Put one tortilla in the pan and fill with a quarter of the sweet potato, black beans and caramelized onions—spread only on one half of the tortilla. Sprinkle with chili flakes.

07 Fold the tortilla in half, cook until the bottom is brown (around 2 minutes), then flip over to brown the other side for another couple of minutes. Remove to a plate.

08 Repeat for the remaining tortillas. Slice and serve!

SERVES 4
50 mins

DJ Format
Behind The Scenes

INGREDIENTS

1 cauliflower
ground cumin
cayenne pepper
1 lb. 2 oz. (3¼ cups) fresh
shelled peas (not frozen)
1 lemon
all-purpose flour
garlic
fresh mint
fresh cilantro
1 container of hummus
1 cucumber
3 tomatoes
1 romaine lettuce
olive oil
vegetable oil
salt and pepper

**THESE LITTLE CRUNCHY
PEA FALAFELS WILL BLOW
YOUR MIND. GREAT IN A
SALAD. GREAT IN A PITA.
GREAT WHEREVER, REALLY.
YOU CAN MAKE A CREAMY
HUMMUS DRESSING BY
JUST ADDING WATER,
OLIVE OIL, AND LEMON
JUICE TO REGULAR
HUMMUS. WHO KNEW!**

CRUNCHY PEA FALAFEL SALAD [★]

01 Preheat your oven to 400°F.

02 Break the cauliflower up into little florets. Place them in a roasting pan. Add a teaspoon of ground cumin and a teaspoon of cayenne pepper. Drizzle over some olive oil, season with salt and pepper, and roast in the oven for 40 minutes.

03 Meanwhile, falafel time. Into a blender add the shelled peas, ½ teaspoon of cayenne pepper, 1½ teaspoons of ground cumin, the juice of half a lemon, a tablespoon of flour, a good grind of pepper, a pinch of salt, 2 grated garlic cloves, and a handful of both chopped mint and cilantro (leave some of each to garnish). Whiz until you have a blended falafel mix. Take a small piece of the mixture and use your hands to form a ball that sticks together. If it doesn't, add a smidge more flour and blend again.

04 Divide the mix into golfball-size balls.

05 Heat ¾ inch of vegetable oil in a deep pan. To check it is hot enough, just put in a tiny bit of falafel mixture. When it immediately starts bubbling, you are good to go. Carefully drop the falafels into the hot oil. Fry for 6–7 minutes, until brown and crunchy on the outside.

06 Set the falafels on some paper towels to absorb excess oil.

07 Get on with your dressing. Into a bowl add 2 heaped tablespoons of hummus, the juice of half a lemon, and a splash of olive oil. Add a splash of water, season with salt and pepper, and mix with a fork. Keep adding water, bit by bit, until you have a smooth dressing consistency.

08 Salad time. Into a bowl add your chopped cucumber (remove the seeds in the middle to make it less watery), the chopped tomatoes, shredded romaine lettuce, the roasted cauliflower florets, and the falafels. Add in the reserved mint and cilantro. Pour the dressing over the top, toss everything together and serve up!

VEGGIE BALTI PIE

SERVES 4
1 hr

Folamour
The Power and the Blessing
of Unity

INGREDIENTS

1 butternut squash (weighing
about 1 lb. 5 oz.)
2 carrots
1 onion
garlic
fresh ginger
garam masala
medium curry powder
ground cinnamon
mango chutney
17 fl. oz. jar (about 2 cups) of
strained tomatoes
plain yogurt
2 x 13-oz. puff pastry sheets
1 egg yolk
vegetable oil
salt and pepper

**THE ENGLISH FOOTBALL-
STADIUM CLASSIC MADE
VEGGIE. BRUSH IT WITH
EGG YOLK TO MAKE SURE
THE PASTRY IS NICE
AND GOLDEN.**

01 Preheat your oven to 400°F.

02 Peel, seed, and roughly chop the butternut squash. Chop the carrots and finely chop your onion, 2 garlic cloves, and a small piece of ginger.

03 Add the onion to a frying pan or skillet with some vegetable oil and cook until soft. Add the other chopped vegetables. Then add 1 teaspoon of garam masala, 2 teaspoons of curry powder, and 1 teaspoon of ground cinnamon. Mix it all in.

04 Add 2 teaspoons of mango chutney. Mix it in, and then add the strained tomatoes. Stir in, and reduce the curry down. Once it is thick, add a generous 1 cup of plain yogurt. Season the balti with salt and pepper, then remove from the heat.

05 Roll out a sheet of puff pastry and lay it into a baking dish. Make sure it comes up and hangs over the sides. Lay some parchment paper on top of it, and then pour in a bag of dry rice to weigh the pastry down. Put the dish in the oven for 12 minutes, then remove the parchment paper and rice, and bake for another 3 minutes.

06 Remove the dish from the oven. The pastry should be dry and partially baked. Spoon in your balti mixture.

07 Roll out the second sheet of puff pastry and place it on top of the pie. Squeeze it along the pie edges to seal. Brush the pie with beaten egg yolk, sprinkle on some salt and then bake for 30 minutes until golden.

08 Cut up the pie and tuck in!

VEGAN BÁNH MÍ WITH MUSHROOM PÂTÉ [VG]

SERVES 4
1 hr 15 mins

Kornél Kovács
Pantalón

INGREDIENTS
2 oz. (½ cup) walnuts
10½ oz. mushrooms
garlic
1 carrot
7 oz. radishes
1 cucumber
white wine vinegar
sugar

01 Toast your walnuts in a dry frying pan or skillet. When done, set aside and clean out the pan with some paper towels.

02 Clean and finely chop your mushrooms and 4 garlic cloves.

03 Heat some olive oil in the pan. Add the mushrooms and garlic, season with salt and pepper, then sauté for about 10 minutes to evaporate all the moisture from the mushrooms.

04 Cool for a few minutes, and then whiz them in a blender with the walnuts until completely smooth. Let cool until the mixture reaches room temperature, then put it in the refrigerator until assembly time to let the garlickyness develop.

05 Grate your carrots and thinly slice or peel your radishes and cucumber (seed this first). Put half of this mixture into a jar with 5 tablespoons of white wine vinegar, 2 teaspoons

10 oz. extra firm tofu
soy sauce
1 lime
baguette
fresh cilantro
olive oil
salt and pepper

A VIETNAMESE CLASSIC, VEGAN-STYLE. PÂTÉ IS KEY TO CREATING AN AUTHENTIC BÁNH MÍ!

of sugar, and 2 teaspoons of salt. Make sure it covers all the veggetables. Chill for at least an hour. Set the other half of the veggies aside.

06   Drain your tofu and slice thinly. Place on paper towels and pat dry.

07   To make the marinade, whisk together 2 tablespoons of olive oil, 2 tablespoons of soy sauce, the zest and juice of 1 lime, 1 garlic clove, and a good grind of pepper. Throw the tofu in a bowl and pour the marinade in. Make sure the tofu is coated before placing in the refrigerator for at least 15 minutes.

08   Add some olive oil to a frying pan and place the tofu slices in it, not touching each other. Fry for a few minutes on each side, until caramelized and golden brown.

09   Cut up a baguette into four pieces. Drain the pickled veggies and chop up some cilantro.

10   Cut open each piece of baguette and layer on the mushroom pâté, tofu, pickled veggies and unpickled veggies, and top with some cilantro!

INGREDIENTS

3 red bell peppers
whole milk
1 lb. 2 oz. (4¼ cups) dried
macaroni
paprika
all-purpose flour
Cheddar cheese
manchego cheese
olive oil
salt and pepper

**CHANGING THE MAC 'N'
CHEESE GAME FOREVER.
MAKE SURE YOUR PEPPERS
ARE NICE AND CHARRED
FOR A GOOD DEPTH OF
FLAVOR IN YOUR MAC.**

ROASTED PEPPER MAC 'N' CHEESE WITH PAPRIKA & MANCHEGO

01   Preheat your oven to 400°F.

02   Add your whole bell peppers to a roasting pan and roast in the oven for 45 minutes, until charred and soft.

03   Remove the peppers from the oven. Allow to cool. Peel off the skins and remove the seeds. Add two of the peppers to a blender together with 2½ cups of milk and a good grinding of pepper. Whiz until smooth.

04   Put the macaroni on (cook for 10 minutes in salted boiling water). Drain.

05   Meanwhile, add 1 teaspoon of paprika and 2 tablespoons of flour to some olive oil in a bowl and whisk together. Start slowly adding the blended pepper mix, whisking as you do this. You should end up with a thick red sauce.

06   Add 3 cups of grated Cheddar and 2 cups of grated manchego. Mix them in until smooth.

07   Once the cheese is melted, add your cooked macaroni. Stir it in. Slice up your remaining roasted pepper and add that, too.

08   Stir everything together, spoon it into a baking dish, and then top it with some more grated Cheddar and manchego. Put the mac and cheese under your preheated hot broiler for 10 minutes until golden and bubbling. Remove from the broiler, spoon into bowls and enjoy!

INGREDIENTS

2 bell peppers (not green)
3 zucchinis
1 red onion
1 cauliflower
14-oz. can of chickpeas
cayenne pepper
garam masala
4¼ oz. (½ cup) dairy-free
coconut yogurt (we use The
Coconut Collaborative)
fresh mint
1 lemon
1 cucumber
garlic
4 pitas
fresh pomegranate seeds
olive oil
salt and pepper

**SUCH A FRESH, SUMMERY
DISH. THE POMEGRANATE
SEEDS AT THE END
PROVIDE THE PERFECT
COOLING BURSTS
OF FLAVOR.**

ROAST VEGETABLE GYROS WITH COCONUT YOGURT TZATZIKI [★] [VG]

01 Preheat your oven to 400°F.

02 Seed and chop your peppers into bite-size pieces. Chop up your zucchinis and red onion in the same way. Break the cauliflower up into little florets. Place the vegetables into a roasting pan. Pour in the can of chickpeas, with some of the starchy water. Pour over a good splash of olive oil, add 2 heaped teaspoons of cayenne pepper, 2 heaped teaspoons of garam masala, a sprinkle of salt and pepper, and mix everything together. Roast in the oven for 30 minutes.

03 Tzatziki time. Pour the coconut yogurt into a bowl. Add a small bunch of finely chopped mint leaves, the juice of a lemon, and the grated cucumber. Grate in a garlic clove, season well and mix it all together.

04 After 30 minutes, remove the roasted vegetables from the oven, mix them about, and then place back in the oven for 15 more minutes.

05 Assembly time. Warm your pitas, then split open. Load each with your spiced vegetables, then tzatziki, then some pomegranate seeds, then some more vegetables, more tzatziki, more pomegranate seeds, and TUCK IN!

VEGGIE PIZZAS (3 WAYS)

SERVES 4

1 hr 20 mins

Cheryl Lynn
You Saved My Day

INGREDIENTS (FOR BASE)

self-rising flour
plain yogurt
salt and pepper
olive oil

RICOTTA, ZUCCHINI & FENNEL INGREDIENTS

9 oz. (1 cup) ricotta cheese
1 lemon
zucchini
fennel
cherry tomatoes
dried chili flakes
fresh basil

GOUDA, KALE & WILD MUSHROOMS INGREDIENTS

kale
fresh wild mushrooms
garlic
fennel seeds
butter
7-oz. block of Gouda cheese

CHERRY TOMATO CAPRESE INGREDIENTS

cherry tomatoes (yellow and red ideally)
garlic
mozzarella
fresh basil

01 Sift 3 cups of self-rising flour into a bowl. Add a very large pinch of salt. Add 10½ oz. (1½ cups) yogurt, bit by bit, mixing it through the flour with a fork. Keep adding it in and mixing it through until it is all in the bowl.

02 Flour a work surface and tip the dough out of the bowl. Flour your hands and knead—first lightly, and then build up the pressure. If it feels a bit wet, just add some more flour. Keep kneading until you have a nice, smooth ball. Add it to a clean bowl and cover the bowl with a damp dish towel for an hour.

03 Preheat your oven to 425°F.

04 Cut and shape the dough into four balls and roll out on a floured surface. You want them thin. Add to two baking sheets lined with parchment paper.

RICOTTA, ZUCCHINI & FENNEL

01 Add the ricotta, the zest of a lemon, a very generous grinding of pepper, and a pinch of salt to a bowl. Mix well. Smooth the ricotta over the pizza bases. Shave very thin slices of zucchini and fennel over the bases. Add a handful of halved cherry tomatoes. Sprinkle on some chili flakes. Add some basil leaves, grate over a bit more lemon zest, and season with salt, pepper, and a very good drizzle of olive oil. Place the pizzas in the oven for 15 minutes until you have a crisp crust. Scatter some more basil over the top and enjoy.

GOUDA, KALE & WILD MUSHROOMS

01 Place some kale in a bowl and cover with boiling water. Break up your mushrooms. Add to a frying pan or skillet with a crushed garlic clove and a teaspoon of fennel seeds. Add a pat of butter and fry the mushrooms down until they are caramelized and dehydrated. Top your pizzas with the fennel mushrooms, kale, and slices of Gouda. Place in the oven for 15 minutes until the cheese is golden and bubbling.

CHERRY TOMATO CAPRESE

01 Add roughly 9 oz. cherry tomatoes to a frying pan with a splash of olive oil and a crushed garlic clove. Cook until the tomatoes are bursting and reduced down. Add the tomato sauce to the pizza bases. Top with torn mozzarella and another 9 oz. cherry tomatoes (halved). Tear over some basil, and place the pizza in the oven for 15 minutes until crisp. Enjoy!

INDEX

THANK YOU

I would firstly like to thank the MOB team: Rupert, Felix, Sam, and Joe. None of this would have been possible without you. Thank you also to Maddie for all of your help with the recipe development. You are a wonderful chef.

I would like to thank my mum and dad for their unwavering support, my brothers, Joe and Sam, for their constant help and advice, and all of my best friends who have been on call at all hours of the day since MOB Kitchen began. Misha, Tommy, Kit, Seb, Milo, Preston, Tom, and everyone else. Thank you, thank you, thank you. Lastly, I want to thank my wonderful girlfriend, Robyn. Your support is overwhelming, I love you.

Next up—MOB's brilliant design team, OMSE. James and Briton, thank you so much for your advice and help making the book look so beautiful!

In relation to *MOB Veggie*, I would like to thank my amazing photography team—Max and Liz Haarala Hamilton on the camera, Charlie Phillips with the best props about, and Alex Gray with the freshest food styling in town. I would like to thank everyone at Pavilion—Steph, Katie, Polly, Helen, Laura, David, and Laura—for making this book happen, and my wonderful agent Cara Armstrong at HHB Agency for being my rock!